On Holy Ground

Sr Anita Woodwell SGS is a priest in the Church in Wales and a Vocations Adviser for the Diocese of Monmouth.

She has been an Ignatian spiritual director for over twenty years and has trained many others in prayer guidance in the UK and overseas.

She is a founding member of the Sisters of the Good Shepherd, an Anglican religious community, and was recently elected its Prioress.

On Holy Ground

Guided Prayer:
a handbook and practical companion

Anita M. Woodwell SGS

Illustrations by Theresa Margaret CHN

CANTERBURY
PRESS
Norwich

© Anita Woodwell SGS 2008

First published in 2008 by the Canterbury Press Norwich
(a publishing imprint of Hymns Ancient & Modern Limited,
a registered charity)
13–17 Long Lane, London EC1A 9PN

www.scm-canterburypress.co.uk

British Library Cataloguing in Publication data

A catalogue record for this book is available
from the British Library

ISBN 978-1-85311-866-1

Typeset by Regent Typesetting, London
Printed in the UK by CPI William Clowes Beccles NR34 7TL

Contents

Acknowledgements

Scripture quotations are, except where noted, from the *New Revised Standard Version*, published by HarperCollins Publishers, copyright © 1989 by the Division of Christian Education of the National Council of the Churches of Christ in the USA, all rights reserved.

Quotations from the *Spiritual Exercises* of St Ignatius are from *A Contemporary Reading of the Spiritual Exercises, A Companion to St Ignatius' Text,* David L. Fleming SJ, The Institute of Jesuit Sources, St Louis, copyright © 1978, second edition, revised 1980.

Appendix 2, 'Guidelines for Distinguishing the Creative from the Destructive' is copyright © Gerald W. Hughes, and is reproduced by his kind permission. An expanded version with clear explanations is to be found in *God of All Things*, Hodder & Stoughton, 2003, pp. 103–12.

Appendix 3, 'Some Guidelines for Discerning How Best to Serve God', was compiled by the author jointly with Enid Morgan SGS, based on the *Jesuit Constitutions*, paragraphs 622–626, and is reproduced here with the latter's kind permission.

Special thanks are due to those who helped with proofreading in the early stages: the Revd Dr Ann Paton, the Revd Sister Enid Morgan SGS, and Christine Woodwell Phenix. Also to three trainees who most helpfully proofread and commented on each chapter as it emerged from my computer: the Revd Janet Bone, the Revd Dennis Richards and the Revd Dr Will Ingle-Gillis. And last, but definitely not least, to Sr Theresa Margaret CHN, whose splendid illustrations so greatly enhance this handbook.

Foreword

In this book, *On Holy Ground,* Sister Anita has done for spiritual direction what Delia Smith has done for cooking! She has provided a much needed practical resource. It is a real gift for clergy and laity who are to accompany others in spiritual direction, as well as for those in other types of Christian ministry.

Today, we are told that organised religion in the West is in decline, but at the same time there is an increasing desire for spirituality. The scriptures – through the ancient practices of *Lectio Divina* and imaginative contemplation – provide a treasure store through which God can speak to each one of us. This process of listening to God speaking to us personally is enhanced by having an experienced spiritual director or *soul friend* to provide the encouragement, insights and promptings that are needed to enable us to hear more clearly what God is saying to us.

Sister Anita has drawn on her years of personal experience to provide a user-friendly manual which will be of particular help to those who are new to this ministry as well as for those who have been doing it for many years. As Delia Smith provides easy-to-follow recipe books, so Sister Anita has provided us with a book that gives step-by-step guidance by pointing out the pitfalls, the difficulties and the challenges as well as showing the joys that are found in accompanying others in their spiritual journeys.

The authority, directness and wisdom contained in this book are the fruits of personal experience and many will benefit from Sister Anita's willingness to share these fruits with others entrusted with the guidance of souls.

+ *Dominic Walker OGS*
Bishop of Monmouth

Introduction

'If only I had been taught that when I started out!'

This is the cry which has many times passed my lips and which has informed every aspect of the courses and programmes I have developed to train others in the art of prayer guidance and spiritual direction. This book is the result of more than twenty years' experience as an Ignatian spiritual director, all too often 'learning the hard way', and its purpose is to help others reach a reasonable level of expertise without having to make too many mistakes along the way. It is a distillation and amplification of the many handouts and course notes I have prepared over the years for those whom I have been training as Ignatian spiritual guides.

Prayer guidance and spiritual direction might be regarded as a 'growth industry' in the Church today, and many excellent books have already been written on the subject. Few, however, address the practical issues, the methodology and the 'how to' of prayer guidance, and none that I am aware of provides a skills-based 'nuts and bolts' approach such as I am offering in this manual. So I sincerely hope that this volume will fill an existing need, and aid both those who are already guiding others, and those who are training to do so.

This manual seeks, without getting bogged down in too much theory, to cover all the basic qualities and skills needed by anyone who dares to stand on the 'holy ground' of another person's experience of God. It looks at the personal qualities and ongoing discipline required if one is to be capable of accompanying others in this way without doing harm. It provides ideas for teaching people how to actually *encounter* God in prayer at a personal level. And, above all, it unravels some essential aspects of prayer guidance, including the 'how to' of discernment, good exploration and intervention skills, identifying the 'heart' of a person's prayer experience, choosing texts for prayer, and dealing with unexpected or problematical situations which might arise in a guidance session.

To avoid confusion, let me say a word about terminology. Many different terms have been used to refer to a person who accompanies, guides and supports another person in his or her spiritual journey. The most common term, despite the fact that it doesn't describe very well what actually goes on in such a relationship, is 'spiritual director'. Other terms frequently used are 'spiritual guide', 'soul friend', and 'prayer guide'.

All these terms, however, denote the work of a person who is helping others to deepen their relationship with God. Regardless of which term is used, the principal objective is to help individuals to experience God's love in a personal way. All the terms refer to someone involved in accompanying others and helping them to understand, appreciate and interpret what the Lord may be trying to say to them. And, whichever term is used, it is essential that such a person recognizes that *God* is in charge – that it is *God* who truly guides and directs, not the 'prayer so-called-guide' or the 'spiritual so-called-director'.

In recent years, in the UK at least, it has been customary to speak of prayer guides as those who are not yet fully trained spiritual directors. 'Prayer guides' may have excellent skills, but typically their understanding and experience of the dynamics of spiritual growth will be less profound than that of a 'spiritual director'. Both, however, do indeed seek to *guide*, at least in a non-directive way, so for the purposes of this manual I shall generally refer to both as 'prayer guides'.

Those being guided may also be referred to by various terms, such as 'directees', 'retreatants', and (in the case of those doing the full *Spiritual Exercises* of St Ignatius) 'exercitants', but for simplicity I shall mostly refer to them as 'persons', 'retreatants' or 'participants'. (For grammatical simplicity, sometimes the female pronoun is used in examples, and sometimes the male pronoun. The specific point being made, though, obviously applies equally to both genders.)

This manual will focus particularly on the knowledge and skills necessary competently to give a 'Week of Guided Prayer' or short residential retreat. This choice is based on the fact that the Week of Guided Prayer is an extremely powerful experience for most who do it, and is readily accessible even to those in full-time employment. Also, from the prayer guide's point of view, the task of guiding others through a Week of Guided Prayer employs all the basic skills inherent in the Ignatian method. Therefore, this form of 'retreat in daily life' is a very good place to start. All the knowledge and skills covered in this manual are, however, readily applicable to any other individually guided event, as well as to most pastoral relationships, and should prove helpful for all those engaged in Christian ministry.

Although ongoing spiritual direction/guidance is somewhat outside the scope of this manual, I recognize that some participants will want regular follow-up support following a Week of Guided Prayer. This may, perforce, involve the prayer guide meeting regularly with such persons over a period of some months, or even years, to support their prayer in the context of their ordinary daily lives. For this reason, I have included Appendix 7, which gives some guidelines for such ongoing direction/guidance.

This book is dedicated to

Sister Pia Buxton CJ

who guided my first and most life-changing
experiences of Ignatian prayer,

and to three sisters in Christ without whose support and
encouragement this book would never have
seen the light of day:

the Revd Dr Ann Paton,

the Revd Sister Enid Morgan SGS

and my sister by birth, Christine Woodwell Phenix.

Some Fundamental Prerequisites for Prayer Guidance

'You are standing on holy ground.'

The door opened abruptly, and the retreat-giver came rushing in, late as usual. She flopped into a chair, panting, and before the retreatant could say anything, launched into a monologue explaining why she was late, and how many other important responsibilities she had. She managed to work a bit of name-dropping into the process, and only after a minute or two took any real notice of the retreatant. She then said, 'Well, we'd better get on with it; I haven't got all day'. Needless to say, the retreatant felt herself to be a nuisance or, at best, an achievement to be notched up on the guide's record of her own importance. The retreatant felt that she was a mere plaything, to be got out of the way as quickly as possible.

Not everyone is suited to the ministry of prayer guidance. Not everyone has the qualities needed to exercise this ministry without harming the very people he or she is supposed to be helping. So it is important to begin by looking at those qualities, skills and attitudes which are essential in anyone who is considering becoming a prayer guide.

Essential Characteristics for Prayer Guides

When I select candidates for training in prayer guidance, there are six characteristics for which I specifically look. (Indeed, ideally, these characteristics should be present in anyone engaged in Christian ministry!)

1 Candidates must be mature and well-balanced individuals, with a healthy self-esteem alongside a sense of unworthiness to exercise the ministry of prayer guidance. Candidates who are inwardly insecure are likely to use the ministry merely to prove their own worth. Those who consider themselves 'God's gift to the Church' are clearly lacking in the self-knowledge and humility necessary to minister sensitively to others.

2 Candidates must take their own prayer life seriously, and sincerely try to spend a certain amount of time in prayer daily. It is first and foremost our *own* experiences in prayer which will give us criteria for recognizing and understanding the Lord at work in another.

3 Candidates must be good listeners. This is not dependent on their personality types! Indeed, some of the most extraverted and bubbly people can, when they choose, move into the sort of 'contemplative listening' which is essential for a good prayer guide. If candidates are good listeners, it is likely that they will already find that others seek them out in order to unburden themselves and talk about their problems.

4 Candidates must be discreet – that is, they must be people who have no tendency to gossip or to divulge secrets. Prayer guidance sessions must be regarded as being absolutely confidential – in essence, 'under the seal of the confessional'. *Nothing* that is said within the sessions may ever be repeated, except anonymously (see the comments on supervision, below) or with the individual's express permission.

5 Candidates must show empathy and sensitivity. If they are too wrapped up in their own lives and problems, it is unlikely that they

will have the capacity for focusing on a retreatant with the necessary attitude of empathy, sensitivity and unconditional love.

6 Finally, though less importantly, candidates must know their way around the Bible. An in-depth knowledge of biblical theology is not essential, as beginners can familiarize themselves with, and make effective use of, lists of appropriate passages for prayer, such as that offered in Appendix 4 of this manual. They should, however, know approximately where in the Bible to find any given book!

So if you are reading this and are uncertain as to whether you possess these qualities, it would be best to consult with an experienced prayer guide or spiritual director, and work on developing them before proceeding!

Skills Needed for Prayer Guidance

The role of the prayer guide calls for a number of specific skills, though if the above characteristics and qualities are present, these skills can generally be learnt. They are:

✔ **Teaching:** The 'listening prayer' inherent in praying with Scriptures is, for most people participating in a Week of Guided Prayer (especially in a parish), a totally new experience. Both in the initial meeting and in the one-to-one sessions, therefore, the prayer guide must be able to explain and teach, clearly and in a reassuring way, the different methods of prayer. (The teaching role of the prayer guide is discussed in Chapter 3.)

✔ **Accompanying:** A prayer guide is primarily a companion to the retreatant, 'walking alongside' that person with genuine love, concern, interest, empathy, compassion and understanding. One of the most important gifts the prayer guide has to offer is that of affirmation and encouragement. (The accompanying role of the prayer guide is discussed further in Chapter 4.)

✔ **Discernment:** Not everything a retreatant experiences in prayer will necessarily be 'of God,' so it is essential for a prayer guide to understand and be able to apply the criteria for discernment, to distinguish between that which is almost certainly of God, and that which may be coming from some other source. (The task of discernment is discussed further in Chapter 5.)

✔ **Exploration:** In order to help the retreatant to appreciate the importance of his or her prayer experience, the prayer guide must have good exploratory skills, and be able to intervene and ask questions, in a non-intrusive and sensitive way, about what the person shares. Most importantly, the guide must be able to recognize and highlight the most significant aspect of the prayer experience described. (The explorative role of the prayer guide is discussed further in Chapters 6 and 7.)

✔ **Guidance:** At the end of each one-to-one session in a Week of Guided Prayer or residential retreat, the prayer guide must give clear suggestions to the retreatant as to how to proceed. This will normally include the giving of one or more new scriptural passages with which to pray, guidelines concerning the use of the passage(s), and often a 'grace to pray for'. So it is important for the prayer guide to have a reasonable 'repertoire' of biblical texts (with which he or she is familiar) from which to choose, to have some sense of what sort of text is called for, and to be aware of the specific grace or graces the retreatant most needs at this moment in time. (This guiding role of the prayer guide is discussed further in Chapter 8.)

It will be evident from the above that most people have a good many skills to learn before they can guide others competently in prayer.

Essential Abilities to Develop

In addition to the skills mentioned above, there are certain personal abilities which are necessary for good prayer guidance (or any healthy Christian ministry). These abilities are interrelated, and can normally be developed if they are not already present, as they are primarily by-products of a healthy prayer life. They are:

➤ **The ability to move, at will, into a state of relative inner stillness.** One cannot listen properly to another without this.

➤ **The ability to step aside from the rush and bustle of daily life into a state of unhurriedness.** (I consider rush to be one of the most useful weapons in Satan's armoury!) If one enters a guidance session feeling pressurized, one's retreatant will pick this up and will be made to feel devalued or even a nuisance.

➤ **The ability to focus on others with a truly contemplative attitude.** This aspect of guiding others may accurately be described as a form of prayer, given that it is a gazing upon God at work in another of his children.

Disciplines Needed by Prayer Guides

Accompanying others on their spiritual journey is an art, not an exact science. For this reason, those attempting to do so must first and foremost be faithful to a disciplined daily prayer routine themselves. Few people are able to maintain such a prayer discipline without setting themselves clear guidelines – which are usually referred to as a 'Rule of Life'. For those who shy away from that term as sounding too rigid, the phrase 'Rhythm of Life' might be more palatable.

The point of drawing up such guidelines is quite simple: without them, our prayer life all too easily degenerates into being a 'pray-when-it's-convenient-or-I-happen-to-feel-like-it' activity. This effectively treats God as a source of self-gratification, rather than as the divine Being who is supremely deserving of our love and worship, and without whom our ministry becomes little more than an amateurish and unprofessional DIY effort.

In drawing up a Rule of Life, it is a good idea to consult with your spiritual director. (It is, of course, axiomatic that all those engaged in guiding others should themselves be receiving such guidance.) There are certain underlying principles which should form a basis for a satisfactory and 'liveable' Rule of Life:

→ Without an adequate amount of prayer time in our daily lives, everything we do will be 'in our own strength' rather than in the grace and strength which God alone can supply. I would suggest that those who guide others in prayer should find at least a half-hour per day for silent prayer, nourished by Scripture in *lectio divina* and/or imaginative contemplation. I am referring to the 'sit still and do nothing but pray' kind of prayer! (Yes, it is possible to pray after a fashion while driving the car or washing up, but the depth and quality of such prayer is not the same and does not normally offer God the uninterrupted attention he needs if he is truly to touch us, heal us and strengthen us in depth.)

→ Prayer guides do not work in isolation from the faith community of the Church, so church attendance is another important aspect of any adequate Rule of Life. It is by worshipping alongside our ordinary fellow Christians and mixing with them in a mutually supportive setting that our private prayer is 'rooted and grounded in reality'.

→ Unless one is a Quaker, one's Rule of Life should include regular reception of the Sacrament of Holy Communion, and normally, for Roman Catholics and Anglicans who are open to it, the Sacrament of Reconciliation. By obedience to the commands of Jesus and the discipline of the Church throughout the ages, we demonstrate that we ourselves are open to ongoing guidance and spiritual growth.

→ Just as retreatants are normally asked to take notes on their prayer experiences, so also it is very beneficial to include in one's Rule of Life the keeping of some sort of prayer journal. Entries need not be made daily, but by writing down a few notes about any significant experiences or insights we may have in prayer (or at other times), we ensure that such experiences or insights are not forgotten or lost.

→ As reflection on experience is the key to all learning and growth, it is a good idea to include, as a short exercise towards the end of each day, what is known as an 'examen of consciousness'. (This should not be confused with an 'examination of conscience'.) 'Examen' can be an un-timed event which, in its simplest form, consists of:

- Asking the Lord to bring to your mind what *he* wants you to remember from the day.
- Allowing your thoughts to wander over the day, and seeing what comes to mind.

- Responding appropriately to each memory which surfaces – for example, with thanksgiving, penitence, prayer for help, etc.

→ As prayer guidance involves guiding others in various forms of retreat, so, obviously, prayer guides should themselves make some form of retreat at least once a year. This should normally be individually guided, as that is the type of retreat most likely to be truly profound and restorative, and it will enable them to be on the receiving end of good prayer guidance. This will also help to build up their repertoires of good texts with which to pray, of which they have firsthand experience.

→ As was said above, it is axiomatic that prayer guides should, themselves, receive regular, ongoing spiritual direction or prayer guidance. My own experience, both of being directed and of directing others, suggests that if the frequency of meeting with one's director is anything less than monthly or six-weekly, many valuable threads are likely to be lost, and the direction session will, therefore, be considerably less worthwhile.

Regular spiritual direction provides one with several important opportunities:

- An opportunity to review and discuss significant experiences or insights you've had (and hopefully written about in your prayer journal).
- An opportunity to get the various aspects of your life into perspective with the help of another who, precisely because he or she stands *apart* from your daily life, can often discern more clearly those patterns and meanings which may be significant.
- Help with discernment when there are decisions to be made. One cannot direct oneself! And the application of the rules for discernment are best done by – or with the help of – someone else who has been trained and steeped in them.
- The encouragement we all find helpful in order to persevere in prayer and in the discipline of keeping our Rule of Life.

→ Few people, when they draw up a Rule of Life, think of taking into account their need for rest and relaxation, but this is particularly important. We are none of us machines who can function endlessly without being switched off, so it can be vital to incorporate into our Rule of Life the ways in which we are going to 'recharge our batteries'. It may be helpful to try to incorporate into one's life the 'six recreational needs':

- **Psychological**: the need for adequate space and the means to manage the stresses in our lives.
- **Educational**: the need to satisfy the desire for lifelong learning.
- **Social**: the need for satisfying friendships and personal relationships.
- **Physical**: the need for sufficient physical exercise to remain fit.
- **Restful**: the need to engage in relaxing activities and to get sufficient rest and sleep.
- **Aesthetic**: the need to nourish the spirit with beauty in all its forms – the visual arts, music, the great outdoors, etc.

→ Finally, it can be important (especially for those who are literal-minded or subject to scruples) to define just when and why their observance of the Rule may and should be relaxed. There are two underlying principles here:

1 Love takes priority over observance. For example, if another person's genuine and urgent need interferes with a time of prayer, that need should first be addressed. The prayer should be resumed afterwards, if and when that is possible.
2 Relaxation of observance is important at times. On a day off or on holiday, for example, it is reasonable to reduce the amount of time spent in prayer. Also, if one is ill, one should relax one's observance of the Rule according to conscience, based on a realistic assessment of one's ability and strength.

Once you have drawn up a Rule of Life, it is a good idea to do a bit of a 'reality check' before discussing and finalizing it with your spiritual director. A Rule which requires no effort on your part is probably not much use. On the other hand, a Rule which is unrealistic and not easily 'liveable' will serve only to discourage and frustrate you. (If you fail to fulfil an obligation today, it will be even harder to fulfil tomorrow.) So do spend some time in prayer and reflection before God as you read over the Rule you have drawn up, and pay attention to any 'niggles' you may have. A trial period is also a good idea. It could save you grief later on.

Ongoing Support and Development

All professionals (and that is what competent prayer guides must be) need ongoing support and opportunities to continue developing their skills. In the case of those who guide others in prayer, I would suggest that such support should include two main elements:

1 Supervision when guiding others, especially for the first few years following one's training. This supervision serves to support and develop the prayer guide's ministry at two levels:

   – that of checking out one's guidance skills (though all discussion of specific encounters must be done anonymously), and
   – that of working through one's own inner reactions and attitudes.

   Supervision typically occurs in two different forms: one-to-one supervision with an experienced spiritual director, and/or mutual supervision among the members of a team working together on a retreat or Week of Guided Prayer. In the latter case, it is important that at least one member of the team be highly experienced.
2 Ongoing learning. This will mean further reading, as well as attendance, whenever opportunity allows, at further training events (though the availability of these will obviously vary according to where one lives).

A Sacred Duty

To sum up, if we are seeking to help others in their personal relationships with God, we have a sacred duty to approach the task with humility, to prepare ourselves for it thoroughly, to maintain our own spiritual and physical health as best we can, and to continue to develop our guidance skills lifelong. Only those who do so are fit to undertake this ministry, in the exercise of which we are indeed standing on holy ground.

2

The Dynamic of Ignatian Prayer Guidance

'Come to me . . .'

It was an altogether new experience for me, as I sat down with the Sister who was to be my spiritual director. Already, in the first prayer time of my retreat, I had had some significant experiences. And, as instructed, I had done some reflection on them afterwards and written a few notes about them, though I didn't fully understand their meaning. As I sat there, lowering my guard and sharing with my director the intimacies of my struggles to relate to God, her gentle, respectful and encouraging response gave me the sense of being truly understood and affirmed. I could feel myself opening out to her, as a flower opens out to the sunlight. And when she began to speak of what I had shared, to affirm its validity and to highlight the most important aspects of it, I felt I had at last found the help I needed to *encounter* God. And that was only the beginning. That retreat became for me the watershed of my life, the point at which I simultaneously discovered God's love for me personally and was enabled to recognize my own worth. It was a truly life-changing event.

✎

Ignatian spiritual direction and prayer guidance are indeed powerful means to bring people to Christ, to foster a deeper relationship with him and to enable whatever inner healing the person may need. Perhaps this is because it is essentially a one-to-one process, focused on the needs of the individual, and because it incorporates a dynamic which is particularly effective in helping people to absorb and appreciate whatever the Lord may be saying or doing within them.

Some who are reading this book may never have experienced an Individually Guided Retreat or Week of Guided Prayer.

I consider it hugely important to emphasize that no amount of *reading about* these will give a person any idea of just how powerful and life-changing such retreats can be. Nor can one adequately guide others in this way without first having experienced such guidance oneself.

To attempt to do so would be comparable to a person who had never tasted wine trying to teach a class on winetasting!

So if you are reading this and have never experienced individual prayer guidance in a retreat or Week of Guided Prayer, **I strongly recommend that you put this book down until you have done so.** Until then, you will not be able to grasp at a meaningful level what this manual is describing.

Dispelling Some Myths

This book is designed as a basic manual for those accompanying others employing the 'Ignatian Method' of prayer guidance. For, despite this method being so widely used nowadays, certain myths about it still linger in some circles (largely among those who have never actually experienced it, or who have had the misfortune to be accompanied by a less competent guide). So I would like to make the following four points:

1 I use the word 'method' rather than 'spirituality' for the simple reason that any **good Ignatian guidance will facilitate the development of the individual's *own* spirituality, whatever that may be and**

whichever of the familiar 'spiritualities' (Franciscan, Benedictine, etc.) it may most resemble.

2 **Ignatian method is very much more than just imaginative contemplation![1]** Ignatius, in the *Spiritual Exercises*, proposes a number of different ways of praying, including what has traditionally been known as *lectio divina*, or 'reflective reading'. It is true that the deepest and most life-changing prayer encounters typically take place when God meets with a person in and through his or her imagination, but there are many different of ways of allowing such an encounter to happen.

3 **Ignatian method is anything but rigid or directive.[2]** When properly used, it is the most flexible and open-ended of approaches. A prayer guide, when giving a passage for a retreatant to pray with, for example, can never predict how the Lord will use it or how it will speak to the person. A good model for what the guide should be doing in any guidance session is that of simply 'giving an occasional tap to the tiller' to help the vessel remain on the course set by God.

4 **The Ignatian method, when sensibly used, is entirely safe.** In effect, it incorporates a built-in safety net in the fact that the prayer guide neither knows, nor tries to tell the retreatant, what experience he or she will have when praying with a passage. This means that God is given a free hand, and will not bring to the surface anything the retreatant is not ready to face or to deal with.

A Fourfold Dynamic

I like to think of Ignatian individual guidance as consisting of a fourfold dynamic. What is notable about this dynamic is that at every point there

---

1 Indeed, there are certain situations in which a good Ignatian guide will *not* recommend imaginative contemplation to an individual. These are discussed in Chapter 8.

2 This 'Ignatian flexibility' can also be seen in the *Constitutions* of the Society of Jesus, in which the typical structure might be expressed in the words 'although normally we will proceed in such-and-such a way, nevertheless, if it seems better to proceed in some other way, we will do so'.

is a further opportunity for the Lord to speak, touch, clarify and deepen insights:

1 **Experience:** The foundation stone of the process is the prayer experience of the individual, normally using a passage set for her by her prayer guide. The Lord will speak to and/or encounter the person in some way during this time of prayer even if, as sometimes happens, she is not aware of it.

2 **Reflection:** The individual should spend a short period afterwards in reflection on whatever prayer experience she may have had, during which she writes a few notes about what happened. This may result in new or deepened insights, as the Lord will continue to speak to her or work within her while she is doing this.

3 **Articulation:** When the individual meets with her prayer guide, she tries to articulate what went on during her prayer time, and what the Lord may have been trying to say to her. As she does so, she will frequently receive further insights into the meaning of the experience.

4 **Dialogue:** The final phase of the dynamic is the resulting dialogue with the prayer guide, during which the guide should be able to affirm the validity of the experience, highlight the most significant aspects of what the individual has shared, and help her to recognize what the Lord may have been trying to do or say. The guide should help the individual to leave this session feeling encouraged and looking forward to her next time of prayer.

Much of what follows in this manual will explore the third and fourth of these phases, as it is in these that the skills of the prayer guide are particularly important. It is also important, however, that the guide be able to teach and explain with clarity to those new to this method the first two phases. For this reason, the teaching role of the prayer guide, together with some of the concepts which need to be taught, will be covered in Chapter 3.

The Week of Guided Prayer

The most powerful and potentially life-changing setting in which Ignatian prayer guidance takes place is the 'Individually Guided Retreat' (IGR). Such retreats may be full-time and residential (typically lasting anything from two to thirty days), or 'in daily life' lasting from a week to a year. The most accessible form, for most people, is the 'Week of Guided Prayer' (WGP), which is non-residential and requires of participants little more than an hour's total commitment per day (apart from travel, should they be travelling from a distance).

As has been explained in the Introduction, the reason for using the Week of Guided Prayer as the basis for a manual on prayer guidance is threefold:

1 The Week of Guided Prayer is a very powerful and enriching experience for most of those who take part in one.
2 It is a form of retreat which is readily accessible even to those in full-time employment.
3 From the prayer guide's point of view, it employs all the basic skills inherent in the Ignatian method. The skills required to guide a person through a Week of Guided Prayer are essentially the same as those required to give a thirty-day retreat (though to do the latter, one requires a much greater knowledge and understanding of the underlying dynamic of the *Spiritual Exercises* – and, indeed, of all spiritual growth).

The Structure of the Week of Guided Prayer

What gives the Week of Guided Prayer its unique character is the fact that it offers to participants intensive individual guidance, while incorporating that guidance into a flexible scheme which does not require them to leave their home or work. Additionally, it offers this in the context of a group of fellow Christians, most of whom are also learning to pray with Scripture for the first time. Whenever possible, this social element is important to foster throughout the week, as it provides the participants with the opportunity to discuss their prayer, encourage each other, and reassure one another that what they are experiencing is 'normal'.

The four main elements of the Week of Guided Prayer are as follows:

1 **Meetings at the beginning and the end of the week:** All participants attend two meetings as an integral part of the retreat.
   - The initial meeting provides the opportunity for the participants to meet one another, and for the prayer guides to introduce the prayer methods which will be used during the week, as well as to defuse any anxieties the participants may have.
   - The closing meeting tends to be more of a celebration. It provides an opportunity for participants to share their most significant experiences of the week, and for the prayer guides to explain the basics of discernment, to teach the practice of the examen of consciousness, and to suggest ways of incorporating prayer into their ongoing daily routine.

2 **The prayer commitment:** At the initial meeting, participants are asked to commit themselves to the following:
   - To pray according to the guidelines given by their prayer guides for a full half hour each day, for five days. This prayer may be taken at any time convenient to them.
   - To spend a few minutes, following the half-hour, reflecting on what happened and writing a few notes about it.

3 **The guidance session:** At some point each day, by mutual agreement, each participant meets with his or her prayer guide individually for up to half an hour. They are encouraged not to worry about what they will say or share, but just to bring their notes with them as an *aide-mémoire*.

4 **The social element:** Throughout the hours during the week when guidance sessions are taking place, there should ideally be tea, coffee and biscuits available for the participants, together with a room or waiting area where they can sit and chat with one another. Typically, this will be the first time in their lives that they have actually discussed with others their prayer and their relationship with God.

Other Forms of Individually Guided Retreats

As has already been said, the guidance skills required to give a Week of Guided Prayer are equally applicable to any form of Individually Guided Retreat. If, however, one is intending to guide retreats of more than a few days (the usual length of longer retreats is eight or thirty days), one should normally have done the full *Spiritual Exercises* of St Ignatius and have undergone more extensive training in the dynamics of spiritual growth and of the *Spiritual Exercises* themselves.

With the basic guidance skills described in this manual, however, one should be able to guide retreatants competently in the following contexts:

◆ **Short Residential Retreats** lasting for up to three days or so. One huge advantage of a residential retreat is the silence which is made possible in that setting. In our modern world of non-stop noise and communications, it can be very difficult to persuade some people to observe the silence, but their experience of God will be immensely more profound and life-giving if they do. Retreatants should be reminded that it is simply not possible to hear God's voice when we are chatting with others, and listening for God's voice *all day, every day* is the object of a residential retreat!

  Retreats of two or three days do not generally require the guide to have an in-depth knowledge of the dynamics of the *Spiritual Exercises*. The normal prayer pattern on Individually Guided Retreats is four prayer times per day, each lasting for an hour (although on a short retreat some retreatants may find a half-hour or forty-five minutes about as much as they can manage). Retreatants who are new to silent retreats may need to be seen twice in the first day, but the fourfold dynamic is the same as that described earlier in this chapter. The retreatant will obviously have up to four prayer times to debrief in each guidance session, and will need to be given the same number of texts for their forthcoming times of prayer.

◆ **Retreats in Daily Life** lasting for a pre-agreed number of weeks. The retreatant will normally spend up to an hour in prayer each day, meeting with the prayer guide once or twice a week. Giving this form of Individual Guided Retreat is more taxing, as the prayer guide may need to suggest as many as seven readings at the end of each session. This could prove difficult (though not necessarily impossible) for a guide who is not well acquainted with the dynamics of the *Spiritual Exercises*. Also, the valuable social element of residential retreats and Weeks of Guided Prayer is usually lacking in retreats done in this way.

Group Guidance

Many directors and prayer guides have experimented with what is sometimes called 'group guidance' in which all guidance takes place in a group setting. The impact of this is similar to that of a prayer workshop, in which teaching on prayer method takes place in a plenary session, the group disperses, and the individuals all pray on the same text (or on a choice of two), and when they reconvene, they have the opportunity to share with the others in the group what went on in their prayer time. The prayer guide may comment or ask questions of individuals rather as they would in a one-to-one session.

While this form of guidance is not altogether useless, it has three very clear disadvantages:

1 Few participants will feel able to share as freely in a group as they would in a one-to-one prayer guidance session, and some will feel unable to share anything at all. Thus they will be unable to receive the individual affirmation and encouragement which is an essential part of prayer guidance.
2 For those participants who may have difficulties getting into *lectio divina* or imaginative contemplation, there is little opportunity to receive the specific help and attention which they would be given in one-to-one guidance.
3 If problems with the method are expressed aloud by one person in the group (or afterwards, informally among the participants), other participants can be adversely affected and discouraged from trying to work through any uncertainties they may be experiencing.

Whenever possible, therefore, I believe by far the best option is *individual* guidance.

A Privileged Task

It should be the privilege and the delight of anyone in Christian ministry to be able to accompany another person through the life-giving experience of an Individually Guided Retreat or Week of Guided Prayer. In doing so, we are truly bringing people closer to God. And by respecting and facilitating all of the component elements of the fourfold dynamic, we will be offering those to whom we minister a life-enhancing, and potentially life-changing, experience.

3

The Teaching Role of a Prayer Guide

'Lord, teach us to pray.'

The retreatant, whom I shall refer to as Jim, came into the room at the appointed time and sat down on the edge of his chair, looking rather apprehensive. This was his first one-to-one session with me, so I explained to him that what would help me most would be to hear what went on in his half-hour's prayer, starting at the beginning. He began to talk, but it very quickly became clear to me that he had not grasped anything about the prayer methods which we had explained at the initial meeting. Instead of praying with just the verses of Scripture I had set, he had studied three whole chapters, and had worked very hard to try and understand the underlying theology. He had come to this session with me as to an exam in biblical theology, fearful that he hadn't come up with the 'right answers' about the meaning of the text. Almost every sentence he spoke began with something like 'I think what this verse means is . . .' or 'I think what God is trying to tell people is . . .'

When I asked Jim if he had noticed any particular verse which spoke to him *personally* or moved him in any way, he looked at me rather blankly, then said he didn't think so. So, having explained once more the difference between *Bible study* and *praying with the Bible* (and having complimented him on his grasp of the former!), I then looked with him at the verses actually set. I began to teach him how to be aware of his own emotions and inner reactions as he read those verses, and how to hear God speaking personally to *him*. By the end of the session he had begun to relax, and when he returned the next day to report on his next prayer experience, he had some deep and personal insights to share with me.

స్మోన

The prayer guide has an important teaching role in any retreat or Week of Guided Prayer, not only with those who are new to 'listening prayer', but also with persons who may have done such a retreat previously. My experience has taught me that one must never assume that a person already knows how to use the time of prayer, even if that was explained very fully and carefully at the beginning of the week or at the initial meeting. It is always important, at every phase of the retreat or week, to notice any misapprehensions or misunderstandings on the part of the retreatant, and to 'remind', clarify and explain anything he or she appears not to have grasped. Mostly, such teaching will concern *method*.

Introducing Listening Prayer

Most people attending an Individually Guided Retreat or Week of Guided Prayer for the first time will never have been taught how to *pray* with Scripture and, for most of them, the idea of actually *listening* to God will be novel and strange. Often, the only form of prayer they will know or ever have experienced will be 'said prayers'. So the first and essential task, at the beginning of any prayer workshop or individually guided event, is to broaden the participants' concept of prayer.

One way of illustrating this is to develop on a whiteboard or flipchart a diagram a bit like this:

A cartoon I like to show at this point is one expressing how I think God must sometimes feel when we pray:

The next question which the prayer guide will need to address, of course, is *how* exactly one can listen to God. It may be helpful to begin to answer this by naming some of the ways in which God can 'get through to us' or speak to us. For example, he can inspire us through the words of another person, through the beauty of nature, through significant experiences in our lives and, most of all, through the words of Scripture. And it is the Bible, 'the Word of God', which we use primarily to hear God speaking and to learn what he has to say to each one of us, individually and intimately.

Now most practising Christians will have had at least some experience of reading their Bibles, and this reading will normally, whether done on their own or in a church group, have taken the form of exegesis or an intellectual analysis of the text – in other words, Bible

Study. While this is an important activity for any Christian, it is nevertheless completely different from the way we use the Bible in the context of 'listening prayer'.

This distinction may be very simply put as follows:

BIBLE STUDY is something we do to increase our understanding of God's ways with humankind.

PRAYER WITH THE BIBLE is something God does, inspiring us, touching our hearts, and healing our hurts through his Holy Word.

Bible study, in other words, involves asking questions about the literal meaning of the text, the author, those for whom it was written, the underlying theological suppositions and such like.

In contrast, **prayer with the Bible** involves opening ourselves to God, and to whatever he may wish to do with us or say to us, by noticing what speaks to us personally in the text, by letting those words and ideas stir our hearts, and by allowing God to encounter us through the events being described.

The prayer guide will, at this point, need to begin to explain the actual 'how to' of praying with Scripture. As with so many things in life, the best way to learn this is by actually doing it. It is necessary to give some basic guidelines, however, before sending people off to pray in this way on their own. (Further teaching will usually be needed in the individual guidance sessions, as few people remember everything that has been explained at the initial session.)

There are two main methods to teach initially:

1 The reflective way of reading Scripture generally referred to by its Latin name, *lectio divina*.
2 The way of inner encounter with God known as 'imaginative contemplation'.

The most helpful way of introducing these will be to explain them in the context of a set time of prayer. This will help the participants to understand the importance of preparation and setting.

Teaching *Lectio Divina*

As *lectio divina* is generally the more accessible method for beginners, it's usually as well to teach this first. In explaining how to get into prayer and listen to God through a passage of Scripture, I generally make the following points.[3]

Preparing for Prayer

✔ During your time of prayer, please do not read books, spend time praying for other people (other than to hand them over to God) or

---

3 There is much more detail given here than what most people will take in during one sitting, so I always give a handout outlining the most essential information for retreatants to take away and read through prior to their first time of prayer. A simple reproducible handout explaining both *lectio divina* and imaginative contemplation will be found (together with PowerPoint presentations) on a CD-ROM, available from the author. This handout is also included in a pack of overhead transparencies, likewise available from the author. See her website at www.onholyground.org.uk.

say set prayers or offices such as Evensong. And, very especially, please *do not do any writing during the prayer time*. All these are good and helpful things to do at *other* times, but they may actually get in the way of *listening* to God. The purpose of this week (or retreat) isn't so much praying *to* God, as *listening to his voice*.

- ✔ Choose a suitable place for your prayer time. Switch off your mobile and unplug your landline (unless there is someone else in the house who will answer it for you and take a message). Your place of prayer should, if at all possible, be quiet and comfortable. It may help you to have some external focus, such as a lighted candle, an icon, flowers, or a combination of these. (Not everyone needs such a focus, but for others it may be very helpful indeed.)

- ✔ If possible, sit in a chair which you find genuinely comfortable. (I find kneeling is an ideal position for prayer – but only for about two minutes!) Some people find it helpful to stand for a moment to begin with, and look at the place where they will be praying, remembering that this is to be the place of encounter with God. Sitting on your bed is OK, provided your room is not as messy as mine usually is! The important thing is to have your back in an upright position, with your head unsupported (unless, of course, you are ill or suffer from a physical disability which would make this difficult).

- ✔ Your prayer time is a solemn commitment to God, so it is vital to take steps to ensure that you persevere in prayer for the entire time you have promised.[4] Your time is a gift you are offering to God and, just as you wouldn't snatch back a gift you had given to a friend, so also you shouldn't be so rude and discourteous as to snatch this gift back from God, even if you can't see what he is doing with it! A further point to remember here is that God *never wastes a minute of the time we give him*. If nothing seems to be happening, it may well be that he is working at the level of your unconscious, preparing you to receive an experience or insight at a later time. So persevere!

---

4 It's OK to look at your clock or watch. But if you prefer not to think about the time at all, I recommend the use of a kitchen timer or other similar device. Personally, I find this freeing – I simply persevere in prayer until the timer goes off!

How to Spend the Time – Lectio Divina:

✔ Begin by taking a minute or two to remember that you are in the presence of almighty God. It may help you to visualize him sitting opposite you in the form of Jesus, or as a pillar of light, or as filling the very air which you breathe. Do whatever works best for you.

✔ Offer the intended time of prayer to God, together with the use of all your faculties. Ask him to help you to listen well, and to be open to whatever he may be wanting to say to you or do within you.

✔ When you feel ready, open your Bible to the set reading, and begin to read it (only the specific verses given) *very slowly indeed*. As you read each word or phrase, notice any inner reactions you may have. For example, you may feel some emotion (even if you don't know why), or have some new insight or idea, or just feel a deeper longing for God. And try to notice *which* word, phrase or idea in the Bible reading seems to have triggered your reaction. If, as happens occasionally, nothing seems to speak to you, it's worth asking God again to show you what he wants you to notice in the passage, and then re-reading it even more slowly. Just occasionally, you might feel bored during most of a time of prayer, but *whatever* your experience, just accept it, reminding yourself that God always gives us the experience we most need.

✔ Each time you notice an inner reaction, pause to reflect on the words which inspired it, and to talk with God about it, as with a very dear friend. Ask him what he wants to say to you *personally* through the words. Now the way in which God typically carries on a dialogue with us is to put a thought, by way of his answer, into our minds. It may look to us like our own thought, but if it arrives quickly, gently and easily, and brings us a sense of peace, calm or contentment, it is very likely from God. If, however, the thought which comes makes us feel disturbed, restless or irritable, that thought probably did *not* come from God!

✔ It is unlikely that every part of the reading will 'speak' to you, and there may be verses which you find disturbing. If so, it is worth asking God to show you *why* you find them disturbing and whether there is anything he wishes to teach you through those verses. Or there may be aspects of the passage which stir up 'Bible study' sorts of questions in your mind. The best thing to do with these is simply to leave them on one side, and go on to those words, phrases or ideas in the passage which *do* speak to you or which move you in some way.

✔ There is no prize for finishing the entire reading in the time you have allotted to prayer! If, for example, the first verse inspires a conversation with God lasting the entire prayer time, that's fine. What matters is that you 'savour' and experience fully as much of the passage as you *do* read, and that you be aware of your inner reactions, and converse with God about his message for you.

✔ If you should find yourself moving into a quieter form of prayer for part of the time, without thoughts or words, that is fine. The important thing is that you maintain your focus on God's loving presence with you.

✔ At the end of the half-hour, thank God for whatever experience you had.

After the Prayer Time:

✔ In order to benefit fully from the time you have spent encountering God, it is important to step back from the experience in order to do a bit of reflection. Ideally, you should take a short break of five or ten minutes before doing so. (This interval of time has been shown to sharpen a person's awareness of what was significant in the prayer experience, while allowing those details which were less important to fall away.)

✔ Then, when you're ready, sit down (perhaps in a different place from where you spent your time of prayer) and write a few notes on what actually happened during that time. It might help to begin by writing down any words or phrases in the passage itself which stood out for you. What insights did you receive as you reflected on them and conversed with God about them? What do you think God may have been trying to say to you or do with you during this time? As you write, you may well find that your understanding of your prayer experience deepens.

✔ It's important to notice what happens to you and the ideas that come to you at other times during the day as well. This is because the half-hour of prayer will have the effect of making you more aware of God's presence and more sensitive to his voice at other moments.

Teaching Imaginative Contemplation

In our culture, unfortunately, many men and women have a deep suspicion of the use of the imagination, *especially* in the context of prayer.

I remember the first time I, myself, was introduced to this method well over twenty years ago. I was seated with a group of about forty other people, and we were being led through a simple imaginative prayer experience. Or, at least, the *others* were. *I* was sitting there frowning with disapproval and refusing to be led! Afterwards, however, as I listened to the others sharing one amazing encounter with Jesus after another – all with 'the ring of truth' about them – I realized that by my refusal to try imaginative contemplation I was probably missing out on something very valuable. Later that day, I went to my room and invited Jesus to come to me through my imagination. He did, and that experience of his presence was one of the most significant moments in my life. I fell down on my knees before him, in tears, unable to look him in the face. That was the beginning of a time of great inner healing and the start of what was to become a very deep and loving relationship.

The value of imaginative contemplation cannot be exaggerated. It is the means whereby we can actually encounter Jesus and be 'discipled' by him now, in the twenty-first century. It is, for most of those who use it, potentially life-changing.

Because of the reluctance of many people to use their imaginations in this way, however, it is generally important to lay very solid foundations before teaching the method itself. I am always careful to do so by making the following points:

◆ Every aspect of our beings, including all our senses and faculties, is God-given. They are held in being by God, and therefore it follows that all of them can be used to relate to God (just as all of them can be used to relate to other human beings).
◆ When we use the imagination in prayer, what we are actually doing is allowing God to encounter us through it. We are, in other words,

opening that aspect of our being to his guidance. We are employing it in the service of our faith.

◆ Imaginative contemplation must not be confused with fantasy. When we use the imagination in prayer, we are guided to imagine *truth* – the truth, for instance, that God loves us and wants to speak to us and guide our lives. So, for example, we know that God loves us and is present everywhere. And as Jesus is divine, he too loves us and is present with us in every place. Therefore, to visualize Jesus standing in front of us or sitting in a chair beside us, gazing upon us with love, is to visualize the truth!

To emphasize this point, I like to show the following illustration:

IMAGINATIVE CONTEMPLATION IS **NOT** FANTASY

RATHER, it is allowing God to use your imagination in the service of **TRUTH.**

◆ Obviously, in the ordinary run of our lives, not everything we imagine comes from God. For example, we are well able to imagine ourselves indulging in sin of one sort or another, and we clearly do not want such influences to 'contaminate' our prayer. So whenever we use imaginative contemplation, we want to ensure that it is indeed God who is guiding it. In order to do this, it is important to take the two steps shown in the illustration below:

To help ensure that it is indeed GOD who is using the imagination:

① Before we begin our prayer, we INVITE God to meet us through our imagination, and to protect it from "other influences".

② We allow our imagination to be guided by a Bible passage which expresses the TRUTH about how God relates to human beings.

Having introduced the use of the imagination, a good next step is to give the participants an actual experience of using it in prayer. The simplest exercise of all is probably that known as 'the empty chair'[5] in which you

---

5 From *Sadhana, A Way to God*, by Anthony de Mello SJ, Doubleday, 1978, pp. 71ff.

visualize Jesus sitting in a chair next to or facing you. Most people can do this without difficulty, and a very moving encounter can often result.

A further step which can give people confidence in praying imaginatively is to lead them in a 'guided contemplation' based on a Gospel passage. For example, I often lead groups using the account of the blind beggar.[6] This requires a subtle balance between giving *enough* detail for the participants to visualize, and leaving the Lord to guide their imaginations at the moment of actual encounter. I usually read the biblical account through once, just by way of reminding the participants of the original story, but I then emphasize the point that *it may happen differently for each of them.* They, for a start, are probably not blind. However, they each have their own needs, and it is these they will be bringing to Jesus.

I then invite the participants to close their eyes and I lead them through the prayer encounter more or less as follows. (Allowing pauses, as indicated by three dots – . . . – is very important (three sets of dots indicates a longer pause). I find that if I am entering into the scene as I describe it, that gives me a better sense of how much time the participants are likely to need at those points.)

'You're standing by the side of a road. Have a look around you; notice what kind of a road it is . . . Now you can begin to hear a crowd of people coming along the road towards you. Turn and look at the crowd . . . There, in the midst of the crowd, is Jesus. He is going to pass right by you. How do you feel about that? . . . This is an opportunity to say to him whatever is on your mind and heart, to ask for his help, his healing touch or his guidance. So take a moment to decide what you most want to say to him when he draws near to you . . . Now, Jesus is within hailing distance of you. So call out to him or, if you prefer, approach him and greet him in whatever way feels right to you . . . Notice how he responds to you . . . Now, say to him whatever you want to say, and see how he responds. He may say something, or speak to you through the expression on his face or through his actions. (Don't worry, however, if you are unable to see his face; a lot of people can't.) . . . You can now spend a few minutes talking

6 Luke 18.35–43.

with him one-to-one . . . . Now when you feel ready, take your leave of that scene, "return to this room", and open your eyes.'

It's a good idea, after leading a group in such an encounter, to ask them to reflect in silence for a few minutes on whatever happened, and to write a few notes about it (for their eyes only). Then, when all have finished writing, individuals may be invited to share with the group about their experience. *Such sharing must, of course, be optional, and no one should be allowed to feel stigmatized by not sharing.*

As people share, it's important to affirm whatever experience each person had, even if he or she said they couldn't 'get into the scene'. It is not actually possible to read or listen to a description of this sort without visualizing it, though there are a few people who, for whatever reason, seem unable to recall it afterwards.[7] In my experience, such people are extremely rare and, in most groups, everyone will have had *some* visual experience of Jesus. What is crucial is that such persons should feel encouraged to go on trying to allow Jesus to come to them in this way. (See my comments on group guidance in Chapter 2. Helping people who have difficulties with visualization is very much easier in a one-to-one guidance session.)

Once participants have grasped the method of imaginative contemplation, have accepted its validity, and have had even a brief experience of encountering the Lord in this way, they are generally well able to pray in this way on their own. I find that it is most beneficial to give guidelines for the time of prayer, and for imaginative contemplation, *after* they have actually experienced it. The first and last sections of the guidelines are identical to those given above under the headings 'Preparing for

---

7 If a person were genuinely unable to visualize anything in his or her mind and to recall it afterwards, that individual would be permanently in the state of a newborn child who cannot make sense of the world around it, and who cannot recognize any of the objects in its field of vision. Each time such people closed and reopened their eyes, they would have to begin learning all over again what their friends and relations look like, what a tree looks like, etc. So *all* normal adults have a visual memory and the ability to access it. If they are unable to do this in the context of prayer, it follows that they may be hindered by something in themselves (possibly unconscious), such as fear of failure or an unwillingness to visualize, lest what they see be untrue.

Prayer' and 'After the Prayer Time'. The following guidelines are those specific to imaginative contemplation:[8]

How to Spend the Time – Imaginative Contemplation:

✔ Begin by taking a minute or two to remember that you are in the presence of almighty God. It may help you to visualize him sitting opposite you in the form of Jesus, or as a pillar of light, or as filling the very air which you breathe. Do whatever works best for you.

✔ Offer the intended time of prayer to God, together with the use of all your faculties. Offer him very especially your imagination, asking him to guide it and to protect it from other influences. Ask him to help you to be open to whatever experience he may wish to give you.

✔ When you feel ready, open your Bible to the reading set, and read through it just once (only the specific verses given), simply to remind yourself of the account. If anything really stands out for you, make a mental note of it, but there is no need to linger over the text unless you feel drawn to do so.

✔ Then, close your Bible and put it to one side. (You will not need to refer to it again unless you're exceptionally distracted, in which case re-reading the passage may help to bring you back to the scene you are trying to imagine.)

✔ Now, enter into the scene described in the passage you have just read. While reading the passage, you will have had a visual image of the place, the people and the event described, so you can begin with that mental picture and just imagine yourself there. 'Walk into the scene' in your mind's eye. Should you find this difficult, it may help you to 'talk' yourself into it, saying, for example, 'I am standing by a roadside. It's dusty and lined by low shrubs . . . Now I can hear a crowd approaching . . .', etc.

✔ Once you are in the scene, let the events unfold more or less as described in the passage you read, but this time interact with God or Jesus, *yourself*. (Don't try to be a character in the passage – just be

---

8 These guidelines, as in the case of those given for *lectio divina*, are more detailed than most people will take in at one sitting. Cf. footnote 3, on p. 24.

you.) For example, approach the burning bush and hear God calling you by *your own name*. Or walk over to Jesus and ask him for whatever it is *you* need at this moment in *your* life. Don't worry if you have only a partial image of him or cannot see his face. What matters is that you have a sense of his presence close by you. *Then see how he responds!* Typically, this is the point in the prayer time when God takes over and guides your imagination. Watch and listen very carefully to whatever you see him do or hear him say, and respond naturally, as when you meet with a close friend.

✔ As in *lectio divina*, the way in which God may well speak to you will be to put a thought, by way of his answer, into your mind. It may look to you like your own thought, but if it arrives quickly, gently and easily, and brings you a sense of peace, calm or contentment, it is very likely from God. If, however, the thought in your mind makes you feel disturbed, restless or irritable, that thought probably did *not* come from God.

✔ Frequently, the actual imaginative encounter may take only a few minutes of your prayer time. This is fairly normal. It's as if God gives us just a brief experience so that we can spend the remainder of the prayer time remembering it, reflecting on its significance and talking with him about it. At other times we may move into a period of simply sitting quietly in his presence without either words or visual imagery. The important thing is to try to remain focused on him and not to allow our minds to wander. (See 'Teaching about Distractions in Prayer', below.)

✔ Just occasionally, you might feel bored and restless enough to be unable to enter into a scene. There may be a number of different reasons for this, but it is important not to allow yourself to be discouraged by it. We all of us have occasional 'dry' prayer times. *Whatever* your experience, just accept it, reminding yourself that God always gives us what we most need or are capable of receiving, and that he will have made good use – at some level of our being – of whatever time we have given him.

✔ At the end of the half-hour, thank God for whatever experience you had.

Explaining the Purpose of the Guidance Session

As was pointed out in Chapter 1, a prayer guide is primarily a companion to the retreatant, 'walking alongside' that person with genuine love, concern, interest, empathy, compassion and understanding, and offering the person affirmation and encouragement. Those participants unfamiliar with individual guidance may, however, harbour some apprehensions about it. At the initial meeting in a retreat or Week of Guided Prayer, therefore, I like to give something like the following illustration to explain the nature of the one-to-one sessions:

> 'This retreat/week will be for each one of you a bit like going for a walk with Jesus. He will have things to say to you, but you may find it difficult to understand him at first. Perhaps this may be because you aren't yet familiar with the language he speaks, or because there are so many voices in your life that you find it difficult to distinguish between his voice and all the others. And in any case you may be so close to Jesus and involved in whatever he is saying that it isn't easy to see your experience in perspective. (Even highly skilled and experienced spiritual directors cannot direct themselves.) So during this week, it's as if your prayer guide will be walking beside you at times, to help you understand and interpret whatever Jesus is saying to you or doing with you, and also to help you to distinguish between what is genuinely his voice and what may be coming from some other source. The role of your prayer guide is that of a companion on your journey. The true "director" during the week is the Holy Spirit!'

I then make the following points:

◆ Don't worry about what you're going to say to your guide during this meeting. Your guide will just chat with you and ask questions which will help you to share about the experience you have had.
◆ The session with your guide is totally confidential. Nothing you say will ever be repeated to anyone else, except with your express permission.
◆ Please bring with you the notes you wrote in your reflection after the prayer time. They are for your eyes only, so we don't want you to

read them aloud, but they may remind you of the different aspects of your experience you will want to share. (It will not help your guide to hear every single detail, so if you've written lengthy notes, we suggest you re-read them and highlight the most significant points before coming, so as to be able to share them in a concise way.)

♦ Even if you feel that *nothing* happened in your prayer time, and that you have *nothing* to share with your prayer guide, that's OK. Trust that whatever your experience (or lack of experience) was, God will have made use of the time you gave him, and your guide will recognize this.

♦ Please don't think that you have to fill the time with your prayer guide. If only ten or fifteen minutes is needed, that's fine.

♦ Your guide will talk with you about whatever happened in your prayer time, and will help you to understand its significance. He/she will also help you to distinguish between those aspects of it which almost certainly came from God, and any aspects of it which may have come from some other source.

♦ Based on what God appears to be trying to say to you or do with you, your guide will select another Bible reading for you to use in your next time of prayer, and will give you a few guidelines on how to enter into it.

Teaching Basic Discernment

The full 'Rules for Discernment of Spirits', as found in the *Spiritual Exercises*, are both complex and subtle. It is important that prayer guides have a basic working knowledge of these, so they will be discussed in Chapter 5. For the purposes of teaching on a retreat or Week of Guided Prayer, however, a simple rule of thumb will normally suffice, at least to begin with.

My practice is to give this teaching at the *end* of the retreat or Week of Guided Prayer, as participants will by then have had enough experience of prayer to be able to relate to what is described. The simple points I make are as follows:

➤ Don't waste time *during* your prayer worrying about whether your experiences, thoughts or insights have genuinely come from God. Just accept them, trusting that most of them will indeed be from him. The time for discernment is not *during* the prayer time, but afterwards!

➤ When you reflect on your prayer time afterwards, you may find it useful to apply a 'rule of thumb' suggested by St Ignatius for identifying what has probably come from God and what may have come from some other source. (At this point I place a sponge and a rock on the table.)

When an experience or thought is NOT from God, it will be rather like a drop of water falling on a rock. There will typically be a 'splash' effect – a sense of disturbance, restlessness, unease or negative feelings.

When an experience or thought IS from God, it will be more like a drop of water being absorbed into a sponge. It will arrive gently and quietly, and will typically leave you with a sense of inner peace and calm.

➤ It is not too difficult to tell the difference between that which truly comes from God during our times of prayer and that which may perhaps have come from some other source. (Other sources may include such things as wishful thinking, unhealed aspects of our being, unresolved difficulties in our personal relationships, or even interference by the evil one.)

The distinguishing characteristics are summarized in the illustration that follows:

BASIC DISCERNMENT

?? ???

(IF) an experience or thought is from God, it will normally:
☀ Arrive gently and effortlessly.
☀ Bring a sense of inner peace and/or joy.

(IF), however, an experience or thought is from some other source, it will usually:
Arrive abruptly.
Bring a sense of unease, inner disturbance and restlessness.

➤ Remember that true inner peace can coexist with suffering. A simple rule is:

For the person who is genuinely seeking God, that which comes from God gives some degree of inner peace and joy, *even when God is asking of the person something painful or difficult.*

➤ Finally, discernment can be a complex task, especially when you're facing an important decision in your life – so it's a good idea to seek the help of a trained spiritual director or prayer guide at such times.

Teaching about Distractions in Prayer

If the two things which are certain in life are 'death and taxes', the one thing certain in prayer – at least at times – is 'distraction'. It is important that participants understand this, so that they will not be discouraged or feel a failure when their minds wander in prayer. Some of the points I consider helpful to explain are:

❖ For most of us, the process of settling into prayer each day will involve a certain 'clearing of the decks' of the matters that are weighing on our minds. I personally find it most helpful to hand over to God in a systematic way each of the main aspects of my life (my religious community, my family, my priesthood, the parishes over which I have charge, and my extra-parochial ministry). As I do so, I will inevitably be commending into God's care those people and situations which are causing me concern. Once I've done that, I am generally in a much less distracted frame of mind, and am better able to focus on God.

❖ Thereafter, the best strategy for dealing with distractions in prayer is twofold:

1 Do not waste energy trying to push the distractions away, as doing so is generally counterproductive.

2 Gently withdraw your focus from the distractions by giving your mind a *different* focus. (It's no good just leaving your mind empty; the distractions will rush back in, like sand into a hole!) The passage of Scripture with which you're praying can provide such a focus, as can gazing at a candle or icon to remind yourself of God's presence with you.

An illustration that shows this strategy is as follows:

What most of us tend to do when we're distracted or worried about something is to focus more on the *problem or distraction* than on God – which betrays an underlying assumption that we must solve the problem *ourselves*, even if we occasionally ask for God's help.

What we need to do, to allow *God* to deal with the problem or distraction, is to take our mind *off* it as far as possible, and to focus simply and solely on God, being sure to *listen*. While we are doing that, God will generally transform the problem or defuse the distraction – often in some way far exceeding our expectations.

❖ Just occasionally, however, a particular distraction may be so persistent that you are unable to remove your focus from it. If this is the case, it may be that the distraction is a matter of such significance that it needs to be *brought into* your prayer. The best way of doing this is to *hold the matter up to God*, inviting him to deal with it as he knows best. It is important, however, as you do this, to keep your focus on the loving presence of God, rather than on the matter itself. Otherwise you will simply end up totally absorbed in it again! Imaginative contemplation is especially useful here, as you can place your distraction – in some symbolic form: for example, in a basket or other container – and hand it over to Jesus, focusing on his face or his presence as you do so. You may well find that he takes it from you and gives you a completely different perspective on the matter as he does so.

Teaching Perseverance in Prayer

Participants who are new to daily prayer may leave the retreat or Week of Guided Prayer all 'starry-eyed' about remaining faithful to this new discipline, and unaware of the fact that it will prove more difficult without the regular meetings with a prayer guide. I consider it important, therefore, to prepare them for some of the difficulties they may encounter. Chief among these, of course, will be the temptation to miss, or at least postpone, their time of prayer. A cartoon I use to illustrate this is the following:[9]

9 As the temptations to postpone prayer will vary according to a person's situation and gender, it can be helpful to invite participants to share their own 'besetting temptations'.

Participants need to understand that such temptations are normal, and that it is important not to give into them, because if they miss prayer one day, it will be much harder to pray the next.

Perhaps the most common obstacle to prayer is the one referred to in the illustration above: 'You haven't got TIME to pray . . .' Most people would cite this as the biggest difficulty they face in trying to pray each day. I like to remind them of the point illustrated as follows:

If you ask people questions about how they spend their time, it soon becomes apparent that they do indeed find time to do those things they *want* to do. 'If there's a programme on the telly you really want to watch, do you find time to do so?' 'If the phone rings and it's a close friend, do you take the time to speak with them?' The moral is that if we genuinely *want* to pray daily, most of us will find that there's plenty of time in the day to do so. It's all a matter of priorities.

Three measures which can greatly help a person to persevere in daily prayer are:

1 Belonging to an Ignatian prayer group, at the meetings of which individuals share what has been going on in their prayer and their lives since the last meeting.
2 Meeting regularly with a spiritual director or prayer guide.
3 Drawing up a simple 'Rule of Life' (See the comments about Rules of Life in Chapter 1.)

As John Donne wrote, 'No man is an island.' (Nor is any woman!) We can all benefit from the accountability and encouragement our fellow Christians can offer us, and the clear objectives provided by a Rule of Life.

Teaching the Use of Examen

At the end of a retreat or Week of Guided Prayer, if not before, I consider it valuable to introduce the practice of daily 'Examen of Consciousness'. This should not be confused with 'examination of conscience', as the purpose is not primarily repentance of sins. Rather, the purpose of Examen is *reflection on experience*, which is the key to all growth (including spiritual).

An example illustrating the need for reflection is that of a child putting his hand into a fire. If the child never reflected on his action for long enough to associate *fire* with *pain*, he would go on throughout life burning himself.

I have already written in Chapter 2 of the 'fourfold dynamic' of Ignatian prayer guidance, and of the role within it played by reflection, and I have described that reflection more fully earlier in this present chapter. In the Examen our prayerful reflection is focused more broadly on the whole of the day that is past – including, but not limiting itself to, the times of prayer.

The simplest form of Examen, as I teach it (and practise it myself), is as shown below:

REFLECTION ON EXPERIENCE
IS THE KEY TO SPIRITUAL GROWTH

EXAMEN is a good way to reflect on your experiences at the end of each day.

① Invite the Lord to show you what he wants you to remember from the day.

② Let your mind wander over the day and respond appropriately to each thought or memory which surfaces.

Teaching in the Context of a Guidance Session

Such teaching as is likely to be needed during individual guidance sessions will be largely the same as that discussed above. The structure of a typical guidance session is discussed in Chapter 4, and specific strategies for dealing with some of the difficulties which participants may encounter are to be found in Chapter 9. So all that needs to be said here about teaching in the context of a one-to-one session can be encapsulated in the following principles:

→ When the person has not understood some aspect of the prayer method (for example, having read the passage only once, without noticing what stands out for her, or having prayed reflectively with an 'event' passage but not entered into it imaginatively), it is crucially important to affirm what she *has* done, and perhaps to describe what she hasn't done as being 'the next step' – so as not to give her a sense that she has failed, or 'done it all wrong'.

→ Whenever giving any teaching in the context of prayer guidance, it is important to offer it with a diffidence and respect which assumes the person may already know what you are saying. For example, it can be thoughtful to begin with words such as, 'It may help if I remind you that . . .' or 'As I expect you remember from the opening meeting, . . .'

→ Finally, you should never, ever assume that the person is incapable of praying in the ways we teach in the Ignatian prayer method. The person should always leave the session feeling encouraged, and wanting to have another try at it. If the person has encountered difficulties in imaginative contemplation, for example, this can usually best be achieved by taking a few minutes to lead the person through a brief experience of imaginative contemplation, as described above.

Imparting Wisdom from on High

Teaching, of whatever subject, must always be based on our *own* understanding, rooted and grounded in our *own* experience. In the case of the teaching on prayer, this means that we must have experienced not only the methods taught, but the difficulties one may encounter in using them. Further, we must have 'at our fingertips' the strategies and tips which we ourselves have found helpful. Only then will we succeed in sharing the methods with others with the humility appropriate to such a sacred task.

4

Listening Skills Appropriate to Prayer Guidance

'Listen, listen to me.'

I had screwed up my courage to share something very personal and precious to me, something I was afraid might be misunderstood or disbelieved. The moment had come, and I began to try to articulate it – but I had barely said a few words when the spiritual director with whom I was sharing leaned back, rested her head against the top of the chair, and closed her eyes. I felt distinctly daunted, but, determined to continue, I pressed on. I tried to share with her a huge shift in perspective I had become aware of, and of an immensely increased inner freedom concerning where and how I should serve God. I found it difficult to articulate coherently, however, and I stammered and faltered at the lack of any response from my listener. When I had finished sharing, she looked at me rather coldly, and said: 'So you aren't really free at all, are you?' I was speechless with astonishment. I felt she had heard her own thoughts and prejudices, rather than what I had shared. I left that session feeling hurt, undermined, diminished and betrayed.

⤳⋇⤸

The need for good listening skills in the context of prayer guidance or any fruitful Christian ministry cannot be overemphasized. Poor listening skills can do immense harm. As we watch the person who is sharing and listen intently with an attitude of unconditional love, we are bestowing upon that person the gift of encouragement. So the quality of our listening is of paramount importance.

The Nature of Prayer Guidance

The context of any prayer guidance session must be prayer. It is in prayer that the guide must approach the session, asking for the grace and guidance of the Holy Spirit that he or she may enter the session calmly confident that God is present and 'in charge'. Whether or not prayer guides choose to pray overtly with the retreatant (see below), they should pray by name for the person they are about to see. My own prayer, prior to a spiritual direction session, is 'Lord, please guide this session and use me as an instrument in your hand, but don't let me get in your way!'

I am often asked, 'What is the difference between counselling or psychotherapy, on the one hand, and prayer guidance/spiritual direction, on the other?' I would identify three main distinguishing features:

1 The relationship formed

In counselling and psychotherapy, it is normal to set certain 'boundaries' on the relationship between the counsellor or therapist and the 'client'. In some cases, these boundaries are so extensive that the client is not permitted to know anything at all about the counsellor or therapist – not where he/she lives, his/her state of life or background. One reason for this, of course, is to permit transference and the therapeutic possibilities this is believed to create.

In contrast, I would suggest that the model for spiritual direction and prayer guidance is that of 'friendship in Christ'. Although the guide should not be talking about himself/herself during a guidance session (except briefly and for good reason; see the Guidelines given below) the relationship should, I believe, be an entirely natural one. If the guide is focusing on the retreatant with genuine love, interest and concern, it is to be expected that a mutual affection will develop, and that in some cases a close and lasting friendship will result.

2 The objectives

The objective of counselling and psychotherapy might be described as helping clients to be more deeply in touch with their own psyches – their emotions, desires, complexes, hang-ups, and so on – in order to work through these with the help of the counsellor or therapist.

The objective of spiritual direction and prayer guidance, by contrast, is to help deepen the person's relationship with God – in other words, to help that individual be more deeply in touch with how much God loves her, and thus to bring her to a state of 'inner freedom' in which she will desire God's will above all else.

3 The method

Counsellors and psychotherapists will typically seek to intervene as little as possible, in order to help the person to be more in touch with themselves and free of immediate outside influences. They will normally try to be relatively anonymous and self-effacing.

Prayer guides and spiritual directors normally engage in a more 'active' style of listening, in order to help the person to be more deeply aware of God in her life. So the guide will affirm, encourage and facilitate all that draws the individual closer to God, and will seek to help her to leave aside the problems and worries which distract her from that task. In this method, it is God himself who will sort out those problems and worries, and will heal whatever may need healing in the psyche, often without the person even noticing, until afterwards, that such healing has taken place.[10]

The Basic Components of a Guidance Session

In each guidance session within an Individually Guided Retreat or a Week of Guided Prayer there are certain components which should be present. These components will not always occur in the sequence given below, and some will crop up more than once during the session, but all are important:

◆ **Welcome the person,** and help her to relax, perhaps asking how she is and how the week or retreat is going for her. It is up to the discretion of the prayer guide whether or not the session begins or ends with 'outward and visible' prayer. Some participants would not be comfortable with this, and in any case it is usually best to pray in silence rather than risk making the person feel inadequate by expressing thoughts which are far from her present state of mind and heart.

◆ **Invite the person to share with you** (in chronological order) what happened during her time(s) of prayer with Scripture, as well as anything significant which may have happened outside of prayer which seems to her to have something to do with what God is trying to say to her. Listen attentively to all that she shares, seeking to identify the 'core experience' of God. (Identifying the 'core experience' will be discussed in Chapter 7.)

◆ **Give a summary of what you believe you have heard,** highlighting those insights or experiences which appear to you to be particularly significant, and affirming those which show the hallmarks of having come from God. (Discernment is dealt with in Chapter 5.) Those thoughts and experiences which, on the contrary, appear to have

---

10 One Jesuit who practised both psychotherapy and spiritual direction is reported to have said that he typically observed as much psychological healing in a person in the course of a thirty-day retreat as he would expect to see in two or three years of psychotherapy.

come from the person's woundedness, resentments or fears should, if possible, be left on one side – unless she specifically asks you to comment on them. The task of the guide is to help the person to place such difficulties in God's hands and to leave them there.

◆ **Give the person the opportunity to comment further,** asking whether there is anything else she particularly wanted to share, and allowing her to clarify what she was saying (especially if she feels you have misunderstood her). You may also wish to ask further questions about her experience (within the time allotted to the session). Make sure you leave yourself at least five or ten minutes at the end of the session to choose and introduce the text(s) with which she is to pray next.

◆ **Choose a passage** for the person's time of prayer. (Guidelines for choosing a passage are given in Chapter 8, and a list of suitable passages is to be found in Appendix 4.)

◆ **If appropriate, suggest a 'grace to pray for'** to be used at the beginning of the person's prayer time, and at other times when she thinks of it. This is a specific request which the person makes to God, arising out of her perceived needs. Provided the grace suggested is fairly open-ended and non-prescriptive, it can be a highly effective way of helping people to dispose themselves to receive those gifts the Lord is wanting to give them. (This practice is dealt with further in Chapter 8.)

◆ **Confirm the time of your next session with the person** (or adjust if necessary).

◆ **End the session on a positive note,** giving the person a sense of your genuine interest and support, and helping her to have positive expectations of what the Lord may say or do in her next time(s) of prayer. Help her to leave with a sense that when God is given a free hand, prayer can be truly wonderful and exciting. Often this can be accomplished by your explanation when giving her passage(s) to her. For example, you might say something like: '. . . when Jesus comes along the road, call out to him and approach him. When he asks you what you want him to do for you, tell him of your needs. I don't know how he will respond; that is for you to find out!' Even if the person is experiencing desolation, it is important that she leaves the session feeling affirmed and encouraged and with a sense of hope. God *is* working within her, and your complete faith in this will help her to remain open to him.

{50}

Guidelines for Listening and Affirmation

Here are some basic guidelines for good, contemplative listening in the context of a prayer guidance session:

1 Posture, Attitude and Setting

Your overall demeanour in a guidance session will have a considerable impact, for good or for ill, on your participant's ability to relax and to be open with you. If you yourself are confident in God's power to guide the session, this will manifest itself in your outward appearance. The following are some guidelines to bear in mind:

- Try to maintain in your heart a positive, caring attitude towards the person to whom you are listening, focusing on what you like and/or respect in him. He will, consciously or unconsciously, pick up your attitude, be it positive or negative.
- Be relaxed yourself, and avoid giving the impression of being in a rush, even if the person has arrived late and there is little time available.
- Ensure that you are seated on the same level as the person, preferably at slightly more than a right angle, enabling natural but not forced eye contact. He may not want to be looking at you all the time, and may find it helpful to be gazing out of a window as he shares.
- You yourself should maintain eye contact with the person most of the time, even if he is not looking at you. If you close your eyes or let your eyes wander, you may give the impression that you are bored and/or not actually listening.

2 Listening

The quality of your listening will likewise have a significant impact on the participant's ability to respond well during the guidance session.

- Listen carefully to what he is sharing with you, *without worrying about how you are going to respond*. What you *say* is not nearly as important as the quality of your attention, interest and empathy with the person.

- As you listen, notice his body language and tone of voice. At times you may find these convey a different message from that conveyed by what he is actually saying. Is he sitting back in a relaxed way, or is he on the edge of his seat? Do you sense that he is at ease, or is there visible tension? (Most spiritual directors find that they have a good sense of 'how a person is' as soon as he or she lays eyes on the person at the beginning of the session.)

- Notice any themes, words or points which come up more than once in what the person shares during the guidance session, retreat or week. These could indicate the direction in which he is being called or aspects of his life which need the Lord's healing touch.

- While the person is sharing, apart from affirming and encouraging, as outlined below, intervene only when there is a good reason to do so. (Guidelines for intervention are discussed in Chapter 6.)

3 Affirmation

The most crucial single response to convey to the person is *affirmation*. As you listen to the participant with genuine and undistracted interest, it is vital to affirm the validity of the experience the person is sharing, and to encourage him to continue sharing without fear. Some guidelines for doing so are as follows:

- By nodding and making 'impressed' sounds while the person is speaking. To listen in total silence can be very unhelpful, as most people need the affirmation and encouragement which comes from *some* vocalization on the part of the listener. The sounds you make must, of course, be natural and sincere – not monotonous grunts at indiscriminate moments!

- By your facial expression, but do not rely on smiling and silent nods as your sole means of affirming and reassuring the person, as he will probably not be looking at you very much of the time.

- By slipping in a word or comment, such as 'Wonderful!' or 'Wasn't that lovely!', if you can do so in a slight pause, without interrupting.

- Just *occasionally*, by *interrupting* a person to stop him racing on to the next thing, in order to help him recognize the significance of what he has just said or described. Sometimes, the very fact that someone speaks hurriedly or appears to be skipping over something may be an indication that the experience in question was particularly profound, but that he is uncertain of your understanding or approval. So it can be very helpful to say something like: 'Might I please interrupt to ask you to repeat *slowly* what you have just said? It struck me as being very important.' Then nod and smile at him encouragingly as he does so, and be sure to thank him for what he has shared or repeated! (Appropriate ways of responding to what you hear and observe are discussed in Chapter 6.)

A Contemplative Role

Prayer guidance is, for the one guiding, a very real form of contemplation – contemplation of God present and at work in his children. It is an awe-inspiring task and a form of prayer, and as such it should call forth from our hearts the loving-kindness, tenderness, compassion and concern which the Lord himself feels for the individual to whom we are listening. When we do indeed listen in this way, our presence cannot but support and help the person with whom we are meeting.

5

The Art of Discernment in the Context of Prayer Guidance

'By their fruits you shall know them.'

The young woman before me was going through a difficult patch in her marriage, and was participating with her husband in a marriage renewal programme. On this occasion, she was sharing with me what had happened in her prayer time the previous day. She had given the full half-hour to the prayer, and it was clear that the experience she was describing had all the hallmarks of a genuine encounter with the Lord. She had heard the Lord speaking to her and calling her to a greater gentleness, rooted in his love for her. It was clear that she had, at that point, experienced an inner peace and contentment in his presence.

As she continued talking, however, I sensed an almost imperceptible change in her attitude. A slight edge came into her voice, and she suddenly said, rather bitterly, 'It's my *husband* who needs to hear this message! When I get home, I'm jolly well going to tell him about it and make him face up to his lack of gentleness!' And she went on in this vein for a minute or so, before it was possible for me to intervene. It took me a while gently to help her to recognize the difference between the inner peace she felt during her actual prayer experience and the disturbance that had entered afterwards, when she began applying the message judgmentally to her husband. Her original experience was indeed from the Lord, but her interpretation of it had begun to be twisted by her own resentments and hurt, and the very lack of a loving gentleness in her intended correction of her husband was clear evidence of this.

Discernment is arguably the single most important task of those who guide others in prayer. No one has a 'hot line to God', and everyone will, from time to time, have thoughts or experiences in prayer (or afterwards) which are manifestly from some other source. I do not propose to discuss the nature of evil nor undertake an analysis of the human psyche in this manual; suffice it to say that we are all of us vulnerable to influences which, whether evil or not, are definitely not of God. So a prayer guide's prime responsibility is to identify (and help the participant to recognize) what in his or her prayer experience has clearly come from God and what may have come from elsewhere.

Some Basics of Discernment

Perhaps the first thing to be said about discernment is that it is a complex task! This is perhaps not so surprising, given the fact that we human beings are so adept at deceiving ourselves and 'rationalizing' in such a way as to canonize our own whims and desires. The complexity resulting from this is addressed very concisely in the *Spiritual Exercises* of St Ignatius, in the section entitled 'Rules for the Discernment of Spirits' – in other words, rules for determining which experiences come from the Holy Spirit, and which may come from another 'spirit', such as self-centredness, unhealed hurts, or the 'evil spirit'.

For all practical purposes, we need concern ourselves with just two main categories:

1 Those experiences which have clearly come from God and bear the hallmarks of his presence and inspiration.

2 Those experiences which may not have come from God. These may come from a variety of sources, such as: the person's unconscious, selfishness, woundedness, or a desire for power or status. Satan is very adept at utilizing such weaknesses in order to lead a person astray!

The basic 'rule of thumb' for discernment which I recommend to be taught in a Week of Guided Prayer or a prayer workshop has already been described fully in Chapter 3. Ignatius' analogy of a rock and a sponge can be used to explain some of the differences usually present between that which comes from God (water being absorbed silently and peacefully into a sponge), and that which comes from some other source (water splashing noisily on to a rock, causing disturbance).

Also in Chapter 3, a further important point was made:

For the person who is genuinely seeking God, that which comes from God gives some degree of inner peace and joy, *even when God is asking of the person something painful or difficult.*

This is an important concept to have in mind when guiding others in prayer, because in some cases it can help to distinguish between the 'pseudo-peace' which someone may experience when she has made a *wrong* decision (having eliminated the genuine call of God which she found too challenging), and the 'genuine peace' which comes from hearing and accepting accurately the voice of God in her life.

The task of discernment may be seen as addressing two interrelated but distinguishable spheres:

➤ Identifying what is and is not 'of God' in someone's desires, thoughts and experiences in prayer, as referred to above, in order to discern what God is trying to say or do with her. This task is fundamental to all prayer guidance. Without the ability to discern what is and is not of God, we will be unable to help the person to hear or understand God's voice. Various aspects of this sphere of discernment will be considered in the following three sections of this chapter.

➤ Helping a person to make a sound decision, based on God's call, which involves, first and foremost, helping her to receive the gift of inner freedom with regard to the options she faces. (This sphere presupposes the previous one, as a prayer guide cannot help a person to discern God's call without the ability to identify what is or is not of God.) This will be discussed under the heading 'Facilitating a Sound Decision', below.

Consolation and Desolation

Before we can hope to help someone competently in either of the above-mentioned spheres, we must first understand clearly the concepts of 'consolation' and 'desolation'. It is worth taking time to reflect deeply on Ignatius' definition of these in the 'Rules for the Discernment of Spirits'.[11]

Spiritual Consolation: This term describes our interior life:

a. when we find ourselves so on fire with the love of God that neither anything nor anyone presents itself in competition with a total gift of self to God in love. Rather we begin to see everything and everyone in the context of God, their Creator and Lord;

b. when we are saddened, even to the point of tears, for our infidelity to God but at the same time thankful to know God as Saviour. Such consolation often comes in a deep realization of ourselves as sinner before a God who loves us, . . . or for any other reason which leads us to praise and thank and serve God all the better;

c. when we find our life of faith, hope, and love so strengthened and emboldened that the joy of serving God is foremost in our life. More simply said, consolation can be found in any increase of our faith, our hope, and our love. A deep-down peace comes in just 'being in my Father's house'.

---

11 *A Contemporary Reading of the Spiritual Exercises*, David L. Fleming SJ, The Institute of Jesuit Sources, 1978, pp. 76–7.

Spiritual Desolation: This term describes our interior life:

a. when we find ourselves enmeshed in a certain turmoil of spirit or feel ourselves weighed down by a heavy darkness or weight;
b. when we experience a lack of faith or hope or love in the very distaste for prayer or for any spiritual activity and we know a certain restlessness in our carrying on in the service of God;
c. when we experience just the opposite effect of what has been described as spiritual consolation. For we will notice that the thoughts of rebelliousness, despair, or selfishness which arise at the time of desolation are in absolute contrast with the thoughts of the praise and service of God which flow during the time of consolation.

All those who guide others in prayer should have these definitions firmly in the back of their minds (if not committed to memory) in every guidance session.

Put more simply:

Consolation is any prayer experience which helps to draw us _towards_ God.
Desolation is any prayer experience which tends to draw us _away_ from God.

Consolation must not be confused with self-complacency, nor must desolation be confused with grief or depression. Desolation is not the only possible source of negative thoughts and experience. A few guidelines for distinguishing between desolation, grief and depression are as follows.

◆ **Desolation** is typically manifested in a disturbance or restlessness, and may well be accompanied by self-centred thoughts and behaviour. It will usually manifest itself especially during times of prayer. There are a number of different causes of desolation, but if you suspect a person is experiencing it, you should gently enquire whether she is giving the full allotted time to prayer. If she is, then she should simply be encouraged to continue doing so and to remember the times of consolation she has experienced previously. You should not, however, attempt to do away with the desolation for her, as it may be serving some important purpose, but you *may* reassure her that it will pass.

♦ **Grief** (whether chronic or acute) will typically be much more specifically focused on a particular loss, and will usually manifest itself not so much in an inner disturbance as in a sense of an aching void. As with other sorts of 'woundedness', the face-to-face encounter with Christ afforded by imaginative contemplation can go a long way towards giving the person a new sense of purpose in life and the courage to move on.

♦ **Depression** is more typically manifested in a much more generalized sense of purposelessness. It will usually permeate all aspects of a person's life, even in the case of those who persevere in prayer and in service of others. If you suspect a person is suffering from clinical depression, you should suggest that she see her doctor – if she hasn't already done so. At the same time, you should continue to support her at the spiritual level, which will of course aid her recovery.

Identifying That Which Is of God

Those new to prayer guidance often feel confused and uncertain when trying to identify what, in a person's prayer experience, is likely to have come from God and what may not have done, and when trying to tell the difference between what is significant and worthy of comment, and what is not. (The latter topic is further explored in Chapter 7.) At this point I will address the former: how to recognize those thoughts or experiences which almost certainly come from God.

There are a few simple clues, 'fingerprints' or 'hallmarks', to look for as you listen to a person sharing his prayer experience. Where the Lord is at work, some or all of the following characteristics will typically be present:

➢ The thought or experience **may arrive with a certain spontaneity and/or rapidity**. The person may report, for example, that a thought was 'suddenly just there'.

➤ The thought or experience **will arrive 'smoothly' and gently**, without any sense of disturbance or disquiet, as water is absorbed into a sponge.

➤ The thought or experience **may feel surprising or unexpected** to the person who is praying. He may say something like 'I was surprised that the Lord would say anything like that to me', or 'I'd never thought of it like that before'.

➤ The thought or experience **will result in an increase of inner peace and joy**. At its best, the person may experience something like his or her 'heart burning within them' (cf. Luke 24.32). At the very least, the individual may experience just a slight glimmer of hope. It is the *nature* of this peace and joy which points to its having come from God, not its *quantity*.

➤ The thought or experience **may result in a positive shift in perspective**. For example, the person may see his situation in a different light, or he may experience a change of heart – towards greater mercy, forgiveness, thankfulness, love, or such like.

➤ The person **may experience 'consolation without prior cause'**. This is an experience of consolation without any discernible predisposing factor, as when the person is feeling a bit discouraged, and then suddenly, for no apparent reason, finds himself feeling much more hopeful and positive.

➤ The content of the thought or experience **will be consistent with Christian faith and morality**. In other words, the impact of the thought or experience will be to move the person towards greater love, forgiveness, selflessness and service of others.

When the person has finished sharing his experience with you, if any or all of the above 'fingerprints' are present, it is important to affirm that you can see God's hand at work in him, and to name the aspect of his experience which particularly stands out as being 'of God' and significant. (The task of identifying the 'heart' of the person's prayer experience is discussed in Chapter 7.)

However, if you're not sure whether any of these 'fingerprints' are present, you may need to ascertain this by asking questions. You should be very careful, if you do so, to ensure that the questions you ask are, as far as possible, *open-ended* – in other words, seeking information from the person, not just a 'yes' or 'no' answer.

Closed questions, requiring a 'yes' or 'no' answer, may give the person the sense that you are looking for one 'right' answer, and may thus elicit inaccurate information. Thus, you should try **not** to ask questions like:

✖ 'Did you feel an increase of inner peace and joy?'
✖ 'Did this thought come spontaneously?'
✖ 'Did you feel a shift in perspective?'

Rather, you should ask questions such as the following:

✔ 'How did you feel at that moment?' (Sometimes, when you ask this question, the person will reply with an 'I *thought* . . . ' answer. In this case you will have to ask again, perhaps using a word like 'emotions' or 'stirrings', and sometimes you have to give an example or two to demonstrate that you're asking for an adjective or descriptive phrase.)
✔ 'Can you describe how this experience / thought / idea "arrived"?'
✔ 'How are you seeing that situation now?'
✔ 'When you heard Jesus speaking those words to you, did you feel surprised or were they what you were expecting to hear?' (Note that offering alternatives is sometimes acceptable, provided you don't give any sense, by your tone of voice, that one is better than the other.)

Recognizing and Dealing With What Is Not of God

I have discussed above the 'hallmarks' or 'fingerprints' one may expect to see when a prayer experience has come from God. It is equally important, however, to be alert to the possible effects of that which is *not* of God. Experiences, thoughts and ideas which are from some other source may bear characteristics opposite to those cited above as 'hallmarks' or 'fingerprints' of God's working in the person. In other words:

➢ The thought or experience **may arrive with a certain jarring abruptness**, like water splashing off a rock. The person may report, for example, that a thought was 'disturbing' or 'disquieting'.

➤ The thought or experience **may simply reinforce a negative or unhelpful thought** that the person was already nurturing. She may report or manifest a sense of discouragement from what she has 'heard' or experienced.

➤ The thought or experience **may result in a decrease of inner peace and joy.** At its worst, the person may experience or manifest gloom or despair.

➤ The thought or experience **will not result in a healthy shift in perspective.** For example, if the person has been harbouring a grudge against someone, it may be clear to you that no healing of that attitude has taken place, or even that the attitude has worsened.

➤ The person **may experience desolation**, the symptoms of which have been described above. Bear in mind, however, that sometimes God *allows* a person to experience desolation, in order to help her to recognize her dependence upon him for all that happens in her prayer.

➤ The content of the thought or experience **may be contrary to Christian faith and morality.** So if the person reports feeling moved to tell someone off or 'pay them back for what they've done', you may be pretty certain that that thought is not of God.

It is also important to be able to recognize the signs of possible inner resistance or 'blocks' (often unconscious) in the person with whom you are working. Some of the symptoms which *might, but do not always,* indicate the presence of resistance are as follows:

➤ The person fails to turn up for a session with you. (But be aware that there might be some perfectly legitimate reason for this, or genuine forgetfulness, and the person really had wanted to come.)

➤ The person reports feeling restless and/or fails to complete the time of prayer. (But remember that failure to complete the time of prayer *may* have been due to circumstances outside his control.)

➤ The person reports that 'nothing has happened' in his prayer time, and you find, on questioning, that his mind was actually elsewhere most of the time. This may indicate a fear of encountering the Lord, or it may simply result from the level of pressure and stress he is experiencing in his life.

➤ The person reports coming up against a block during the time of prayer. (When the person is actually *aware* of a block, it is relatively easy to deal with this; see the 'all-purpose strategy' described below.)

➤ The person expresses fear or seems unable to 'let go and let God' in his prayer. (Again, the fact that the person is *aware* of this fear or inability to trust renders it relatively easy to deal with, using the 'all-purpose strategy' below.)

➤ The person is unable or unwilling to use his imagination and/or to involve himself in the event being imagined. Such a difficulty may arise from prejudice or adverse indoctrination, but it may equally indicate resistance rooted in a fear of encountering the Lord. (See the strategies suggested in Chapter 9.)

➤ The person expresses a sense of distance from God. This may be due to inner resistance, or it may simply be an expression of 'how he is' in relation to God at the present time. It can help to ask the person to invite the Lord to give him a sense of his close and loving presence.

In my own experience, the most common causes of resistance tend to be:

◆ Fear of what God may ask of the person, and/or
◆ An image of God as a vengeful judge or something equally negative.

Although it may not be helpful to comment on what you perceive as possible resistance in the person, it is important for *you*, as the prayer guide, to notice it and bear it in mind. In your exploration with the person, it might help you to verify whether or not resistance is involved by asking the following sort of questions:

✔ 'You mentioned feeling frightened. Have you any sense of what might be causing that fear?'

✔ 'Can you recall what was going on within you when you decided to cut the prayer time short? In other words, how you were feeling or what you were thinking?'

✔ 'When you found you couldn't continue imagining the event, did you have a sense that there was something more that *should* have happened?'

It is not, however, essential to be able to identify the cause of the resistance, nor to analyse its nature. The golden rule in prayer guidance is to leave it to *God* to show the person whatever it is he or she needs to see and is ready to deal with. This is because the healing which God typically offers, unlike psychotherapy, does not necessarily involve bringing the problem or its cause to the surface of the person's consciousness. Thus, God's healing is much gentler and safer.

If you suspect that there might be resistance at work in the person, an 'all-purpose strategy' which can effectively deal with it (and will do no harm to anyone) is simply to give the following 'grace to pray for'. (The use of a 'grace to pray for' is discussed in Chapter 8.)

'Ask the Lord to deal with anything within you which might be hindering his approach.'

If there is any danger of the person feeling 'got at' or reacting in a paranoid way to such a suggestion, it would be wise to add that you don't *know* whether there is anything in him or her hindering God's approach, and that this 'grace to pray for' is just to ensure that all channels are open to him.

(Some examples of situations involving apparent resistance or blocks, with other suggested strategies for dealing with them, will be found in Chapter 9.)

Facilitating a Sound Decision

Before a sound decision can be made with regard to God's will for a person, that individual needs to be in a state of what is technically referred to as 'indifference'. Indifference, in this use of the word, however, does *not* have the sense of 'not caring' or 'having no opinion or preference about something'. Rather, it means that one is 'like a balance at equilibrium' (to use St Ignatius' analogy) and is trying to be 'as free toward the object of my choice as I possibly can be'.[12]

---

12 *A Contemporary Reading of the Spiritual Exercises*, David L. Fleming SJ, The Institute of Jesuit Sources, 1978, p. 44.

Thus, a better description of this state of mind which is so essential to making a sound decision is 'inner freedom'. A person in this state may well be aware of having a preference for one option over the other, but is nevertheless inwardly free to choose whichever one should seem to be God's will. If the person is truly in tune with God, his or her overruling desire will be to choose that option which will *best serve God* – in other words, that which will be to his greater glory. (The assumption is that all the options being considered are *good* and that any of them could be pleasing to God; for Christians there is 'no contest' between good and bad options!)

In practice, then, the following steps need to be taken to help a person to make a sound decision:

1 The first thing a prayer guide may need to do in order to facilitate someone facing a decision is to encourage that person to make sure of the relevant facts and to gather adequate information about each option. This may help to rule out certain options, while highlighting the validity of others.

2 Once the genuine options have been identified, the guide should help the person to *take his or her mind off the decision,* and to focus simply and solely on God, praying for the grace of inner freedom concerning the matter to be decided. It is as the person encounters God and is enfolded in his love that a right perspective on the matter to be decided will normally come. (The strategy illustrated in Chapter 3 under 'Teaching about Distractions in Prayer' is equally valid when it comes to leaving a decision in God's hands.)

3 When the person seems to have reached a state of relative inner freedom concerning the possible options, various strategies may be offered. Strategies suggested in the *Spiritual Exercises* (especially helpful when there are two clear options involved) are:

- A careful weighing of the consolation and desolation which result from reflecting on each of the possible options. An effective way of proceeding with this strategy is to suggest to the person that he spend an entire day imagining that he has definitely decided on one option, then the next day imagining that he has definitely decided on the other. By noticing the desolation or consolation he experiences on each of these days, it may become clear which one is God's call to him.

- A 'four columns exercise', consisting of listing (slowly, prayerfully and reflectively) the advantages of one proposed decision, followed by the disadvantages, then the advantages of the other proposed decision, and finally the disadvantages of that one. (Although some overlap will obviously occur between the advantages of one and the disadvantages of the other, by treating them in separate columns, factors may surface which would otherwise be over-looked.) Having completed this exercise it is important to sift the contents of each column carefully, to eliminate the more trivial considerations and highlight the more weighty ones. The end result can frequently give great clarity as to which option will be to the greater glory of God.

- An imaginative contemplation, doing one or more of the following:
  - Imagining oneself advising another person facing the same decision in the same circumstances.
  - Imagining oneself at the point of death, looking back to discover which decision one would wish to have made.
  - Imagining oneself, after one's death, standing before Christ as Judge, and discussing with him which decision one should have made.

- A weighing of the valid options against the criteria outlined in Appendix 3: Some Guidelines for Discerning How Best to Serve God. These can often help a person to take into account important factors he may have overlooked.

4 After it has become reasonably clear to the person which option she should choose, there remains one important step in the process: she should pray for the Lord to confirm her decision. Such confirmation may take many different forms, and in the case of certain decisions – such as those involving vocation – will depend on the judgement of others. Generally speaking, however, if the right decision has been reached, the person will experience a degree of inner peace about it, even if she is uncomfortable with certain aspects of what implement-ing the decision will involve.

As will be clear from the above, it is unlikely that you will be able to facilitate the making of a major decision within the time span allowed in a Week of Guided Prayer or a weekend retreat. If a person is facing a major decision during such a brief event, ongoing guidance and support will almost certainly be needed in the days and weeks which follow. Given that major issues can surface for people when they set aside more time for prayer than usual, some form of follow-up will ideally be available for participants after all such events.

Sifting and Winnowing

The task of discernment might well be compared to a sorting out of the wheat from the chaff in a person's prayer experience. God's word comes to all of us who are listening, but it comes through the filter of our mind-sets and prejudices, hang-ups and wounds, so always there is the danger of mishearing or misinterpreting the word we have heard. A failure to recognize this danger can lead to the worst sort of religious fanaticism. So our responsibility as prayer guides is to ensure that the person we are accompanying hears and responds to the voice of God in its purest and most life-giving form.

6

Intervention and Exploration Skills

'And their eyes were opened.'

John was a middle-aged businessman who had previously been an officer in the Navy. He had just begun his first ever Individually Guided Retreat, and after explaining to him how to enter into a passage imaginatively, I had sent him off to pray with Luke 5.1–11, the account of the calling of the first disciples. When he returned that afternoon, I could tell he was feeling discouraged. He sat down rather heavily and sighed, and then immediately said 'Well, I'm afraid nothing happened.' Undaunted, I asked the usual questions to ascertain that he had indeed prayed for the full time allotted, and that he had begun by reading the passage. It quickly became clear that he had had no problem at all moving into the passage imaginatively. He had found himself in a beached boat – evidently his own – and then Jesus had come along and had got into the boat with him. And there they had sat, facing each other in silence. But nothing further had happened.

So I asked John to describe the scene in more detail, and to tell me about the boat. He proceeded to do so, describing it as 'wooden with two seats'. I then asked whether it had sails. 'No.' 'Did it have oars?'

'No.' 'Well, how was it propelled? Did it have a motor?' 'No.' As he replied to these questions, I could see the realization dawning on him just how strange the boat was. I then said to him, 'So your boat had no means of propulsion. Perhaps it's not so surprising that you weren't going anywhere?' And I suggested that for his next prayer time he return to his boat and sit with Jesus, discussing the meaning of this state of affairs – and asking what Jesus might be showing him about his own life.

To cut a long story short, by the end of the retreat John had concluded that his life was going nowhere, and had accepted that God was calling him to missionary service.

ᕙᕗ

Exploration and intervention are an important part of competent prayer guidance, without which many valuable and God-given experiences would be lost or discarded for lack of recognition of what they mean. So prayer guides should be able to notice not only what retreatants describe, but also what is missing. They should have the skills to elicit from retreatants their inner reactions, details of how the prayer time unfolded and information which may have been overlooked, as well as to reflect with the retreatant on the meaning of the resulting whole.

The Purpose of Interventions

As has been explained in Chapter 4, the listening which takes place in prayer guidance tends to be more 'active' than that in pastoral counselling. The prayer guide's objective is not primarily to help people to be more in touch with *themselves*, but rather to foster and encourage their relationships with *God* through teaching them prayer method and affirming their efforts. So although a good prayer guide will intervene only when there is a valid reason to do so, there are quite a few such 'valid reasons'. Some of these might be:

✔ In order to clarify your understanding of something the person says if you're not sure of the meaning. This should take the form of a *tentative* question, allowing the person to correct you if necessary, such as:

- 'Are you saying that . . .?'
- 'Is it that you're feeling . . .?'
- 'Have I understood correctly that . . .?'

✔ In order to help the person focus on her *experience* rather than her *thinking*. If she seems to be sharing an analysis of her prayer without saying what happened during the prayer time (e.g. without relating anything about the visual content or what stood out for her in the passage she prayed with), it could be helpful to ask something like 'Could you describe to me what actually went on during the half-hour?' or, if imaginative prayer, 'Could you describe how you visualized the scene and what actually took place?'

✔ In order to answer (very briefly) a question implicit or explicit in what the person says, if it is relevant to her relationship with God. For example, if she says 'I find it hard to pray to God; I can only pray to Jesus', you might want to comment that Jesus *is* God, and that it is fine to address any of the three persons of the Trinity.

✔ To reassure the person when she doubts that her prayer is valid/genuine/correct. For example, if she reports that her prayer was a failure because she was distracted, it would be important to reassure her immediately that we all suffer from distractions in prayer. (In this context, I frequently ask people whether they gave the full half-hour or hour to God; when they say they did, I reply, 'Well done! God won't have wasted a minute of that time, as long as you *tried* to stay focused on him.')

✔ To help the person to recognize the meaning and significance of what she has just described, or to appreciate its importance. Some useful questions to achieve this might be:

- 'How did you feel at that moment?'
- 'How do you feel right now, as you remember that moment?'
- 'Please could you recount that experience in a bit more detail, describing the surroundings, who was there and so on?'
- 'When you heard Jesus speaking those words to you, how did you feel?'

As has already been mentioned in Chapter 5, these sorts of question may also prove useful to help you to discern what, in the person's prayer experience, may or may not have come from God.

✔ To highlight and affirm experiences or insights which seem particularly significant and/or which bear the hallmarks of having come from God. You may want to repeat a word or phrase yourself, or say something like, 'Would you mind saying that again? It strikes me as being really significant – something you need to hold on to.' Such affirmation is hugely important, especially when working with someone relatively new to prayer. For the person to be asked to repeat something – or to hear the prayer guide repeat it with emphasis, respect and/or awe, followed by a pause – will feel very reassuring and will also help the person to reflect more deeply on its meaning.

✔ To express understanding and compassion, especially if the person confesses a sin or failing. (Confessions are dealt with more fully in Chapter 9.)

Some Guidelines for Interventions

Intervention must, needless to say, always be undertaken with great sensitivity and respect – never abruptly, or without regard for the thinking process of the person who is articulating his prayer experience in your presence. The following are a few fairly general guidelines for intervening during a person's sharing:

❖ Do not speak of yourself or your own experiences in prayer *unless* you feel that to share something would *genuinely* help the person, or if the person specifically asks you. But, even then, be brief! It is normally appropriate to share your own experiences only in situations such as the following:

  – To give a specific example of one of the ways in which God relates to us.
  – If the person has confessed a sin, in order to reassure him that we are all sinners and that you do not think any the worse of him for what he has confessed.

- To reassure the person that everyone has distractions, dry periods and other difficulties in their spiritual lives.

❖ Never change the subject, unless the person has 'wandered' and is no longer talking about his experience of God. This will sometimes happen when there is a painful experience in the person's past with which he has not yet come to terms, and about which he is obsessing. In such a case, the following guidelines may prove helpful:

- You can reassure the person that areas within us which God wishes to heal do tend to come to the surface when we are face to face with him. You can then go on to explain how to hold the painful memories before God in openness and trust, while focusing on *him*, rather than on the memories.
- Although such issues do indeed need God's healing touch, *prayer guidance is not counselling,* and one must gently steer the person away from those issues and back to his relationship with God here and now.
- *It is through letting go of the issue and focusing on God instead that the person will find healing.* So you may want to say something like: 'I think I've heard enough now to understand what you're describing. Could we now put that on one side and return to considering what God may have been trying to say to you during your prayer time? (Further strategies for helping in this sort of situation are considered in Chapter 9.)

❖ Do not give advice, nor try to solve any problems the person may share with you, unless there is some very *practical* suggestion you think might help. For example, if the person is trying to pray at a time when there are lots of interruptions, you might want to suggest that he take his prayer time at a different time of day.

❖ If the person is experiencing desolation in his prayer, although you will want to make 'compassionate sounds', do not try to console him or 'cheer him up', apart from assuring him that it is not unusual for such experiences to happen in prayer. Such times can prove constructive provided the person perseveres in praying as usual.

The Purpose of Exploration

Exploration may take place in the form of an intervention while the person is sharing, but usually the best time to explore and discuss the person's prayer experience is *after the sharing has finished.* This is because the prayer guide will not have a 'whole picture' of what is going on until that point. Indeed, to begin discussing and exploring the meaning of someone's experience prematurely can sometimes leave the person thinking or feeling something like 'Wait a minute, I'm coming to that; give me a chance!'

Exploration should never be undertaken merely to 'fill the time', and in some instances the person will have given such a clear report of her prayer, her emotions and her sense of what was most significant, that to ask further questions would be quite inappropriate – and even disrespectful of the completeness of the person's sharing. More often, however, it is necessary (and helpful) to spend a few minutes discussing what she has shared.

There are a number of reasons for such discussion and exploration:

1 For purposes of discernment (as has already been discussed in Chapter 5).
2 In order to help the person to become aware of potentially significant details in the experience she has described, as in the example given at the beginning of this chapter.
3 To help you to identify the 'core experience' within the prayer time being described. (Identifying the heart of a person's experience will be discussed in Chapter 7.)
4 To help the person recognize for herself the significance of something she has shared.
5 When you see what might be signs of 'resistance', in order to help the person to be in touch with it and to identify the underlying cause. (The signs of resistance have been discussed in Chapter 5.)
6 In order to explore what is *absent* from the account a person gives of her prayer experience. One example is given at the beginning of this chapter, but others might include

    – A lack of any reference at all to the text (in *lectio divina*).

- A skipping over of potentially significant elements or a lack of any visual description (in an imaginative contemplation).
- An absence of any involvement in the scene (in an imaginative contemplation).
- And (perhaps most importantly), the absence of any dialogue with God/Jesus or, in imaginative contemplation, a failure to approach Jesus or be approached by him.

Some Guidelines for Exploration

As in the case of interventions, exploration should be undertaken in a spirit of love, reverence and great respect for the person and for what God has already been doing in her. When pointing something out, it is especially important to speak in a way that assumes the person may already have recognized for herself what you are saying. So, as has already been noted in Chapter 5, exploration and discussion of the prayer experience of a person needs to be undertaken with considerable care and sensitivity. In particular:

✔ Care must be taken not to convey to the person any sense of there being a 'right' answer. Questions could be prefaced with the words, 'Just to help me understand what the Lord may have been trying to do/say in what you've described, might I ask . . . ?'
✔ Questions should be open-ended whenever possible. This usually means asking questions which cannot be answered simply by saying 'yes' or 'no'. Some examples have been given above (interventions which could at times be helpful during a person's sharing), and also in Chapter 5 (questions which could help you to discern whether resistance may be present). Examples of questions more likely to be useful in the discussion which *follows* the person's sharing might be:

- 'What sense do you have of what God might have been trying to say to you in that experience?'
- 'Might I ask you to recount the visual aspect of your experience in a bit more detail, describing the surroundings – who was there and so on?'

- 'What impact do you think this prayer experience might have on your daily life?'

✔ Sometimes, however, when other means of eliciting this information have failed, it may be necessary to ask a closed question, such as:

- 'Did you feel close to Jesus at any point during your imaginative experience?'
- 'Did you have any sense that Jesus was aware of your presence?'

✔ As with every other aspect of prayer guidance, the explorative discussion which follows the participant's sharing should serve to affirm and encourage her prayer – whatever happened or didn't happen. So it is important to interject positive comments into the conversation with sufficient frequency to make it clear that you see the person's experience as having been valuable.

Sanctified Interest

Whatever intervention and exploration we engage in while listening to others' prayer experience should flow naturally from our genuine interest in them and in God at work within their lives, and should be guided and tempered by our respect for the sacredness of their experience. Although we should not intervene or explore simply to satisfy our own curiosity, nevertheless, if we truly love God and the person in front of us, we will want to understand better what has happened between them. And it will be our joy and delight to be able, at the end of a session, to say, in essence, 'I see God at work within you.'

7

Identifying and Summing Up the Heart of a Prayer Experience

'Do not be afraid, it is I!'

As I listened to Mike, the young man in front of me, recounting what had gone on during his prayer with Isaiah 61.1–3, I found myself feeling overwhelmed with details, any of which *could* have been significant, but none of which had quite the 'feel' I had come to expect of a real encounter with the Lord. I realized that what I was hearing was Mike's *thoughts about* what the text meant and his *thoughts about* the various words and phrases which had caught his attention and had stirred his interest. He raised various questions which were going through his mind as a result of his reading of the text, and began to discuss liberation theology in the light of the passage.

As soon as I could do so, I said to him, 'Well, it sounds to me as if you found the text very interesting. But I wonder if we could go back and consider the *feelings* which were stirred up as you prayed with it. Might I ask at what point in your prayer time you felt closest to God?' Mike looked slightly surprised, paused for a moment, and then said 'Well, I suppose it must have been the words "release from darkness . . ." When I read those words, I suddenly had a sense of a warm light – sort of glowing – all around me . . . . But I don't know what that meant; I expect it was just my imagination.'

Further questioning on my part established the fact that Mike had felt a very deep sense of peace and of the Lord's presence with him at that moment, and had become inwardly still – at least until his distrust of the experience had 'kicked in'. So I was able to say to him with some conviction that that sensation of light, far from being 'just a figment of his imagination', had been the heart of his prayer experience. It had truly been an encounter with the Lord. And we went on to explore together why the Lord might have given him that sensation of light, and what it might mean.

One of the most important aspects of prayer guidance is to identify what I like to call the 'heart of the experience' or 'the core experience'. I define this as being the moment during a time of prayer when the greatest closeness to God was experienced – the moment of closest encounter – or, at times, the moment of greatest insight or shift in perspective. The person sharing, as in the above example, will not always have recognized it as such, so it is essential that the prayer guide have the skills and understanding needful to do so.

I typically find that for most trainees in prayer guidance this identification of the 'core experience' is the most difficult part of their training. They often seem unable to distinguish between the various aspects of the experience being recounted, and will frequently home in on an interesting but peripheral experience, rather than 'the heart' of what has been shared. It is for this reason that I am awarding to this matter an entire chapter of its own.

Emotional Reactions at the Heart of the Experience

In order to recognize the heart of someone's prayer experience, it is essential to be taking in not only the *content* of what the person is sharing, but also *how* the person shares it, and the reactions he or she reports or manifests when doing so.

To give some sense of what this means, it can be instructive to consider a few biblical accounts of personal encounters with God:

- In the account of Elijah's encounter with God on Mount Horeb (1 Kings 19.9–18), the 'core experience' was clearly the moment of hearing a 'still, small voice' (RSV) or a 'sound of sheer silence' (NRSV), to which Elijah responded by covering his face with his cloak – an expression of deep awe. A neophyte prayer guide listening to this account might, however, be tempted to explore the more dramatic elements of earthquake, wind and fire. This would clearly be a mistake!

- In the account of the call of Isaiah (Isaiah 6.1–8), it is the moment of seeing 'the Lord sitting on a throne, high and lofty', surrounded by the heavenly hosts, which is the heart of Isaiah's experience. And his response is to express feelings of deep unworthiness: 'Woe is me! I am lost, for I am a man of unclean lips, and I live among a people of unclean lips; yet my eyes have seen the King, the LORD of hosts!' And it is *this* experience (not so much having a hot coal pressed to his lips – to which no emotional response is recorded) which enables him to say 'Here I am, send me!' Again, a neophyte prayer guide might feel tempted to explore Isaiah's sense of unworthiness, rather than that central encounter.

- Moving to the New Testament (John 1.45–51), there is the account of Nathanael being brought to Jesus in a somewhat sceptical frame of mind. The heart of his encounter was when Jesus expressed prior knowledge of him by having seen him under a fig tree (presumably referring to something no one else could have known). The response evoked in Nathanael is astonishment, followed by a complete shift of perspective expressed in the words: 'Rabbi, you are the Son of God! You are the King of Israel!' To a neophyte, Jesus' pronouncement that Nathanael will see more amazing things in the future, might look like the 'climax' and therefore the 'core experience', but it is not.

- A final example is the encounter the two disciples had with Jesus on the road to Emmaus (Luke 24.13–35). Although they were with Jesus and close to him for a period of time, it was the moment at which he broke bread with them that they recognized him. Only with *hindsight* were they able to say 'Were not our hearts burning within us while he was talking to us on the road . . .?' It is clear, therefore, that the 'core experience' was the recognition of Jesus in the breaking of the bread, and that it was this (rather than the actual walking along the road with him) which enabled their moment of greatest closeness to him.

In all these accounts, there are certain factors present: 1) a close encounter with God/Jesus, 2) an emotional response, and 3) an outward expression of that emotion, either in words or in actions or both. In the context of a prayer guidance session, too, when these elements are visible, one may be reasonably certain that one is hearing about the closest or most significant moment of a person's encounter with God, the heart of the prayer experience.

The ways in which a person may convey an emotional response are many and varied. Some of the more common manifestations of such a response are as follows:

❖ The most obvious, of course, is that the person may choke up or shed tears as she is speaking to you.
❖ There may be a longish pause in the person's sharing, indicative of an attempt to hold back tears.
❖ The person may give a shake of the head or have a facial expression manifesting an element of disbelief.
❖ The person may manifest a deep peace or joy which she finds difficult to articulate.
❖ The person may report having felt 'moved' in some way during her prayer time; for example, having been in tears, having felt great joy, etc.
❖ You may notice a theme or experience bringing consolation which recurs either in the course of the prayer time or over a longer period.

Obviously, an emotional response to something *other* than what has taken place in the person's encounter with the Lord is unlikely to be the core experience. For example, I have frequently worked with recently widowed persons, who quite naturally shed tears during their prayer time as they recall their loss. The heart of their prayer experience, however, is usually the moment when they find themselves face-to-face with Jesus and/or enfolded in the compassionate love of God, which typically brings them some comfort or increase of inner peace.

The Visual at the Heart of the Experience

In a prayer guidance session, it is also important to be listening to the 'picture' described by participants – to be alert, in other words, to the visual element of their experience. This is especially (but not exclusively) relevant when the prayer being described is an imaginative contemplation. Even in *lectio divina*, however, a person may experience significant visual elements.

Some of the 'visuals' which may help to indicate the heart of the person's experience, especially when she has evoked an emotional response, are as follows:

❖ The person may have experienced Jesus/God as either being close or drawing close to her, or she may herself have drawn close to Jesus. She may or may not have envisaged precise details, and the visual aspect of the experience may even have been extremely vague; what matters is the 'spatial closeness' experienced.

❖ The person may report having experienced eye-contact with Jesus. This can be very significant, and is usually accompanied by some degree of emotional response.

❖ The person may have received or 'seen' something symbolic – even if she doesn't understand what it symbolizes. Care must be taken with images, however, as not *every* image is significant, especially when a number of them have been experienced in the same prayer time, or when the person is 'playing with the imagination' (see Chapter 9). The image may or may not have been accompanied by words, but if it is the core experience one may expect that the person will probably have some sense of its importance and/or of its meaning.

The Other Senses at the Heart of the Experience

Experiences mediated through the other senses may also, at times, be significant and give some indication as to the 'heart' of the prayer. For example:

- ❖ The person may report feeling the Lord's hand on his head or shoulder, or having felt himself embraced or held by God.
- ❖ The person may report having felt a breeze or a wind.
- ❖ The person may report noticing a certain scent or smell, such as 'a woodsy smell', or 'a freshness in the air'.
- ❖ The person may, during the imaginative experience, have been offered something to taste.
- ❖ The person may hear the voice of Jesus/God speaking, or may hear music. At times, a person may report some hymn or song 'playing itself' in his mind while he prays. (It can be worthwhile trying to find out what the words were, even if the person couldn't recall them at the time, as they may relate to what God has been trying to say to the person by other means.)

The Intellect at the Heart of the Experience

Although the emotions usually give a better indication of the heart of the experience, the Lord may also 'encounter' the person through the intellect. So it is likewise important to notice such experiences as the following:

- ❖ The person may have received some new or deepened insight.
- ❖ The person himself may believe something significant to have taken place.
- ❖ The person may have experienced a deepening of his faith, or of his grasp of basic Christian beliefs.
- ❖ And, perhaps most significantly, the person may have experienced a shift of perspective or attitude. Such a shift may, in itself, *be* the 'core experience' of a prayer time, or it may have *resulted from* the 'core experience'. In either case, it is – as has been discussed in Chapter 5 – one of the typical signs of God at work in someone.

Other Signs to Look for

There are other possible indicators which are worth watching out for, which may sometimes (but not always) alert you to a significant or 'core' experience. Ones I have come to recognize over the years include the following:

* The person may drop her voice and speak in something of an undertone while recounting the experience. This may be due to the presence of emotions, or perhaps to the fact that she is unsure of the validity of what she is sharing or of how you might receive it.
* At times a person may rather hurry over a highly significant experience, rushing on to whatever came after. This is sometimes simply because she herself senses the importance of the experience and is frightened to share it with you, for fear you will think it of no account.
* Sometimes it is a recurring word or theme which will indicate the heart of the prayer experience. For example, the person may mention a particular thought which entered her mind more than once during her prayer time, or she may use a particular word several times as she shares her experience with you.
* The person may lower her gaze or look away when describing a significant experience. This may indicate deep emotion, or simply that the person is 're-living' the experience as she shares it with you.
* Other gestures are also worth noticing, such as the person taking hold of a cross (if wearing one), gripping her Bible, or stroking the back of one hand with the other. These may indicate that the person is feeling an emotion, 're-living' an experience, or is simply deep in thought.

Identifying the Heart of the Experience

Identifying that moment of greatest closeness to God which constitutes the 'core experience' is not always simply a matter of watching and listening attentively. There are times when you may feel uncertain, after a person has finished sharing what happened in his time of prayer, just what the heart of the experience was. It is then that you will need to apply good exploration skills by asking a few questions.

Many of the questions which can be useful for identifying the core experience will be the same as you might use for the purposes of discernment (see Chapter 5). (Obviously, if a prayer experience does not bear the hallmarks of having come from God, it will not be the core experience!) Some other questions which can be useful for this purpose are the following:

- ✔ 'If you had to choose one verse, phrase or word from this passage as being the most significant for you, which would it be?'
- ✔ 'What would you say was the most moving moment in the prayer time you have just described?'
- ✔ 'At what point during that imaginative encounter did you feel closest to Jesus?'
- ✔ 'If you could re-live that experience, which part of it would you most want to go back to?'

Summing Up

After the person has finished recounting whatever happened in his prayer time, it is very important to affirm *immediately*, at least in general terms, the value of his experience. You should then give a brief summary of what you consider the most important moments or insights to have been, *even if you have been highlighting them as you go along*. This final brief encapsulation of the 'core significance' of the prayer time about which the person has just shared is important in order to:

- ➤ Encourage and reassure the person that God is indeed working in him.
- ➤ Remind the person of any specific insights and/or experiences he needs to remember and cherish.
- ➤ Help *you* to identify what sort of passage might be most helpful to give the person for his next prayer time. (Choosing a passage is discussed in Chapter 8).

In summarizing and encapsulating the heart of the person's experience, you can't go far wrong if you do *both* of the following two things:

1 Make a general comment affirming that the prayer time was both valid and valuable. For example:

   - 'Thank you for sharing that with me; it's always a privilege to see God at work in another person as he clearly has been in you.'
   - 'What a wonderful prayer time!'
   - 'Well, I know you felt a bit disappointed at this prayer time, but it seems clear to me it was actually very valuable.'

2 Then go on to say what you felt was the 'core experience', beginning with something like the following:

   'It seems to me that the most significant moment/insight/aspect of the experience God gave you in this prayer time was . . .'

By being certain to do *both* of these things, you will be helping to ensure that the person is in a positive frame of mind to receive the next passage(s) you give him with which to pray, and that he leaves your presence feeling affirmed and encouraged.

Treasure Hunting

If I have made the task of identifying the heart of a person's prayer experience sound a bit like hunting for treasure, that is no accident. I do indeed see it that way. As prayer guides, we are all the time seeking to unearth the gems of experience and insight that the Lord will have planted in the person whom we are accompanying. Even if such gems are not immediately discernible, we will know that they are there; finding them is simply a matter of patience and of faith. And each time we do succeed in finding them, in bringing them to the surface, and in helping the person before us to recognize their significance, we will have done that person a very great service indeed.

8

Choosing and Presenting Biblical Texts

'This is the way; walk in it.'

It was the last day of my retreat, and I had shared with my director, as usual, what had been coming up for me in my latest times of prayer. I had described to her, in particular, an exceptionally vivid experience of the entry into Jerusalem, with tender moments observing Jesus fondling the colt. Out of this had come a conversation with Jesus, in which he spoke of such moments as 'precious time wasting', and encouraged me to value similar moments in my own life – as, for example, when my cat comes to me, wanting to be cuddled. The final prayer time (with 2 Corinthians 12.7b–10) was a particularly reassuring one, in which Jesus named to me my strengths, including my passionate love for him and my passionate desire to serve his people. Almost as an aside, he had reminded me not to mind too much what others thought of me.

After listening to all this, my director had little to say, and I went off, still glowing with the Lord's tenderness and reassurance which had been at the heart of the prayer experiences I had just shared. As I prayed with the new passages my director had given me, however, I found that every single one seemed to refer to *weaknesses* and to not caring what others think of you. (They were Hebrews 4.14–16, Matthew 12.1–8, John 10.22–30, and Luke 8.49–56.) I felt positively 'got at' and very upset indeed by the time I prayed with the last passage. I felt my director had completely ignored the precious encounters I had had with Jesus, as well as the message of reassurance he had given me, and had homed in *exclusively* on the peripheral reminder concerning what others thought of me. This really spoilt the end of my retreat, and left me with a bitter taste in my mouth.

Although the choice of texts for prayer is by no means the most important aspect of a prayer guide's task, it is important that such texts be chosen carefully, and in a way which reflects the most positive aspects – that is, the *core* – of the prayer experiences a participant has shared. Your choice of text can be a powerful help to the person – or a real hindrance.

The Purpose of Praying with Biblical Texts

Apart from the obvious fact that the Bible, as the inspired Word of God, is uniquely suited to facilitating an encounter with him, there are also other reasons for proposing texts for a person to pray with:

- ◆ By choosing for the person a particular sort of text with a specific theme, you are able to facilitate the person's moving in the direction the Lord seems already to be indicating.
- ◆ By asking a person to pray with only certain verses of a biblical passage, you can effectively 'narrow down' the focus of the person's prayer, thereby encouraging greater depth of thought and experience, and less 'dilution' from filling the mind with a number of differing concepts and ideas.
- ◆ At times, the text you choose can help the person to spend more time deepening his or her understanding of one particular message. (Care must be taken, though, not to give a text which could be perceived as 'getting at' the person – as in the case cited above – nor to give such

a restricted passage that the person finds it difficult to hear other messages the Lord may be wanting to give.)

◆ When a person prays with specified passages, it is much easier for the prayer guide to discern where the Lord may be at work in that person – and where he *doesn't* seem to be working or where there might perhaps be blocks – by noting which aspects of the text do *and do not* speak to the person.

The Universal Dynamic of Spiritual Growth

Before considering the question of how to choose passages, it is worth saying a few words about what I think of as 'the universal dynamic' of spiritual growth. This dynamic might be defined as *the sequence of experiential discoveries through which the Lord leads people who are open to him closer to himself*, as encapsulated most particularly in the *Spiritual Exercises* of St Ignatius. (This dynamic was not, it is important to note, invented by St Ignatius. It was he, however, who recognized it and wrote it down with greatest clarity, thus producing, in the *Spiritual Exercises*, one of the most powerful instruments for personal conversion and discernment the world has ever seen.)

If I had any doubts about the universality of this dynamic, or about the ability of the Lord to lead a person through it regardless of my own expectations, these were laid to rest on a weekend retreat many years ago when I was directing a middle-aged professional woman. To my astonishment (and delight), I saw the Lord recognizably lead her, in just two days, through each and every phase of the *Spiritual Exercises*.

Now, clearly, that experience was unusual. In the course of a Week of Guided Prayer or a short residential retreat, the Lord does not typically lead people through much of the dynamic of the *Spiritual Exercises*.[13] Generally, especially in the case of those who have never made a retreat or Week of Guided Prayer before, their 'agenda' will consist simply of

---

13 There is one school of thought which considers it valuable to deliberately guide a person through the full dynamic of the *Spiritual Exercises* in an eight-day retreat, but my own experience would suggest that this can feel extremely 'forced' on account of the time limit, and can inhibit the agenda *God* has for the retreatant at that point in his or her life.

encountering the Lord in depth and discovering how much he loves them.

Nevertheless, it is worthwhile, even for those prayer guides who have not themselves made the full *Spiritual Exercises*, to have a rough idea of that 'universal dynamic' or 'sequence' in the back of their minds. Just occasionally, this knowledge may assist them in deciding what passage might be helpful to give a person next.

The phases of this dynamic are as follows:

❖ **A grounding in God's love.** This phase is absolutely essential to all further spiritual growth. If the person has not had a 'felt experience' of God's love for her personally, she will be unable to benefit from or respond adequately to the subsequent phases.

❖ **Awareness of sin.** This awareness of sin can only bear fruit in genuine repentance if it is seen against the backdrop of God's infinite love and mercy. Only thus can it call forth an unqualified repentance – that is, a repentance untainted by excuses and self-pity.

❖ **A personal call to follow Jesus.** Having experienced God's amazing love and forgiveness, the person is ready to hear a personal call to service (or a renewal thereof).

❖ **Personal 'discipling' by the Lord.** The person then 'accompanies' Jesus through his life and ministry (by means of imaginative contemplation), and is taught and trained directly by him in the ways of inner freedom and sacrificial self-giving. During this stage, most people experience an ordering (or re-ordering) of their lives in accordance with God's will.

❖ **Suffering with Jesus.** Nowhere is God's love manifested more clearly than in the passion and death of Jesus, so the person next 'walks beside him' to Calvary. During this phase, many people are once more acutely aware of their own sinfulness and unworthiness.

❖ **Resurrection and new life.** In this phase, when the moment is right, the person encounters the risen and victorious Jesus, and becomes more than ever aware of her own call to spread the good news.

❖ **Self-oblation grounded in thanks and praise.** Finally, the person experiences the wonder of God's love in all creation and in every aspect of her life, and is able to offer herself to God as never before, with no strings attached.

In choosing a text for a person, especially when she is quite simply enjoying God's presence, it can be useful to ask oneself whether there is any hint of one of the above phases in the experience she has just shared, or indeed in the previous prayer encounters she has had during the retreat or week. If so, it can be helpful to give her a passage which will support her in that phase. It is important to note, however, that *you should not deliberately move a person on to the next phase unless and until you hear and observe aspects of that next phase coming up in the person's prayer.*

Some Guidelines for Choosing Texts

When choosing texts for prayer, the prayer guide should always remember that the selection of a passage is *not* the most important part of his or her role in guiding others, and that God will use the passage given, even if it is not the best that could have been chosen. (See Chapter 9, point 20, concerning a person having prayed with the wrong passage altogether.)

Many trainee prayer guides, however, seem to find the selection of passages a daunting task, so I offer a few guidelines below which might be helpful:

- ✔ If, while listening to the person, a passage or verse from the Bible comes into your mind, make a mental note of it, or (if *absolutely necessary*) jot it down very quickly, without, as far as possible, interrupting your attention to and eye contact with the person sharing.
- ✔ The most fruitful time, in my experience, for deciding what sort of text to choose is when I am in the process of 'encapsulating' what I consider to be the core experience of the prayer the person has just recounted to me. And it is indeed that 'heart of the person's experience' which should clarify for you what the Lord seems to be saying or doing in that individual – and, therefore, in general the sort of passage which will best support that.
- ✔ It is also helpful to note what the person appears to *need* most at this time (based partly on your own perception and partly on the desires and needs expressed by the person himself). For example, if he has

expressed a longing to be closer to Jesus (or a difficulty in approaching him), you might want to offer him a text such as the account of blind Bartimaeus (Luke 18.35–43), in which he may be helped by others to respond to Jesus' invitation to draw near.

✔ It is normally best, in a short retreat or Week of Guided Prayer, to lead people into imaginative contemplation as quickly as possible, by giving them 'account passages' to pray with, and giving them clear guidelines for getting into them (see below). This is because the deepest and most life-changing encounters with the Lord typically take place in this method of prayer. **It is 'felt experience' which touches and heals whatever may be amiss in a person, not 'intellectual thoughts', however inspired the latter may be.**

Once a person is accustomed to receiving visual imagery, or to envisage Jesus/God present with him regardless of the passage he has been given, it is fine to give a '*lectio divina*'-type passage, as he will have a 'felt experience' all the same.

✔ Don't be in a rush to come up with passages. People typically appreciate the care with which you choose a passage for them, as manifested by your need to reflect on the matter for a minute or two. I generally say to the person something like: 'Right; I'll just take a minute or two now to pray and reflect on what passage(s) might be best to give you for your next prayer time(s).' (On rare occasions, if you should feel really stumped or if there is a shortage of time, you can ask the person to telephone you later, by which time you will have selected the relevant passages.)

✔ Trust your instincts as to what passage to suggest, but unless you're very experienced in prayer guidance, *you should always look at the passage yourself before suggesting it.* It may be there are thoughts expressed in it which could *hinder* the person at present, in which case you may need to exclude certain verses or choose a different passage altogether.

✔ When a person has experienced imaginative visual content or symbolism in his prayer, it is usually advisable (and safest) to choose texts which pick up on that imagery or experience, rather than ones which necessarily follow a specific thought or insight that he may have been given. (See the example cited at the beginning of this chapter.)

✔ Although the Lord will use whatever text the person prays with, your choice of text can greatly hinder the person's ability to be open and accessible to him. So beware of giving:

- Texts which could come across to the person as 'preachy', admonishing or rebuking. It is normal for someone, especially when new to this method, to be asking himself why you have given him a particular passage, so anything containing even slightly judgmental elements could inhibit his openness to God and undermine his trust in you.[14]
- Texts which could give the impression that you are trying to prove a point you have previously discussed with the person. This, too, can cause the individual to feel 'got at'.
- Texts containing involved theological discussion. Such texts tend to keep the person at the level of the intellect (as in Bible Study) rather than the level of felt experience. And it is within the latter, of course, that a truly life-changing encounter with God will usually take place.

✔ In certain cases, you may feel led to suggest that the person pray again with a passage. This is known as 'repetition', and is a normal part of longer retreats. I find repetitions to be less helpful during a short retreat or Week of Guided Prayer, but times in these when they *could* be useful are:

- When you have a strong sense of the text itself having elicited something especially significant which would be difficult to deepen with a different text.
- When you and/or the person sharing have a sense of an 'unfinished encounter', especially in an imaginative contemplation.
- When the encounter elicited by the text has been hugely significant, powerful or moving for the person.
- When the person shares with you his own sense that he needs more time with the text.

---

14 The exception to this rule is the case of a person making the full *Spiritual Exercises* who is in what I have described as the 'awareness of sin' phase – known as the 'First Week' of the *Exercises*.

✔ It is important to note that a different method is called for when guiding someone who appears to be emotionally unstable or mentally ill. In the case of Weeks of Guided Prayer and open retreats, you do not necessarily have the opportunity to screen those attending, so it is important to know how best to 'contain' and support such people.

The first rule in such cases is *not* to propose imaginative contemplation. The safest way to facilitate such a person's prayer is to propose either a few verses from a very innocuous Psalm (preferably relatively devoid of imagery),[15] or a 'biblical mantra' such as the Jesus prayer.[16] For those who are happy with it, praying the rosary is considered to be very safe.

✔ Even if you are very clear as to what the 'heart' of the person's prayer experience was, and even if you have a fair idea of the sort of passage which would be most likely to help, you may need to make use of one or more aids in order to decide on which specific passage to suggest:

- To begin with, you might find it helpful to consult Appendix 4 of this book, which lists some Scripture passages suitable for prayer; remember, though, that most passages have more than one application, so it may be worth looking in several different 'categories' on that list.

- If you have a key word in your mind as a result of listening to the person's experience, or if you know what passage you want to propose but cannot remember where to find it, a concordance can be invaluable.

- You may wish, as you become more experienced in prayer guidance, to compile your own list of texts suitable for prayer – preferably ones you yourself have prayed with at some point.

---

15 Parts of Psalm 119 (such as verses 1–8, 33–37 or 169–175) are particularly appropriate, being somewhat repetitive and without much imagery.

16 The 'Jesus prayer' is a simple prayer, usually repeated over and over like a mantra, based on the cry of Bartimaeus in Mark 10.47. In its full form, it is as follows: 'Lord, Jesus Christ, Son of the living God, have mercy on me, a sinner.' In the Eastern Orthodox churches, it is often said using a simple knotted woollen rosary, simply to 'measure' a period of time spent praying it.

Some Guidelines for Presenting Texts

It is not generally enough simply to give a Bible reference to the person, especially when guiding someone new to praying with Scripture. It is important to help prepare her for the prayer experience she will be having. There are several ways in which you can do this.

◆ *Throughout* a Week of Guided Prayer, at *every* guidance session, I consider it important to explain to the person *fully and in detail* the normal pattern of a prayer period – that is, settle comfortably, get in touch with God's presence, ask for a 'grace', open Bible, etc. (Many people forget from one day to the next!) (See full explanations in Chapter 3.)

◆ It is likewise important, when giving an 'event' passage to someone who is relatively new to imaginative contemplation, to give that person clear guidelines for getting into the event. For example, you might say something like: 'You will be standing by the roadside, and you will hear a crowd approaching . . . Jesus will be drawing near . . .' (Be careful, though, not to set up any specific expectations concerning what will actually take place between the Lord and the person. When describing the 'moment of encounter', just say something like: 'Once Jesus is near enough, call out to him whatever you feel you need or want to say, and then *see what happens, see how he responds . . .*')

◆ When giving the reference for the passage you have chosen, it is wise to repeat it twice to ensure that the person has written it down correctly. Be especially careful to distinguish between, for example, 1 Kings and 2 Kings, between the *Gospel* of John and 1 or 2 John, and so on. If a person does pray with the wrong passage, God will use it, but it is much better that she prays with the right one!

◆ It's a good idea to remind the person to look *only at the verses you have suggested*, to avoid a 'dilution and dissipation' of the experience, and to help her not to move into 'Bible study mode'.

◆ Finally, it is important to make it clear to the person *that you do not have any specific expectations or foreknowledge* concerning what experience God will give her when praying with the passage. You should encourage her simply to *trust whatever comes.*

Proposing a 'Grace to Pray For'

One of the most useful and effective tools a prayer guide or spiritual director can employ is that which is colloquially referred to as 'the grace to pray for'. This is a grace which the person requests from God at the beginning of her time of prayer. In the context of a Week of Guided Prayer or a short retreat, one might not necessarily propose such a grace to a person, but it is a very good idea to do so when a particular area of need surfaces for her.

Why is this simple tool so effective? I like to explain it thus:

'If you try to hand me a present, but I remain sitting here with my arms crossed, you can't really give it to me. We're all a bit like that when God wants to give us graces and help us with things. Yes, he knows what we want and need, but until we are open enough to *ask* him for them, it's a bit like sitting here with our arms crossed. *Asking* for what we need (at least in general terms) is like stretching out our hands to be *able* to receive what God is wanting to give us.'

Those who have served as prayer guides or spiritual directors for any length of time will attest to the fact that God does indeed give the graces for which people pray. So it is well worth familiarizing yourself with the idea and having an understanding of the type of grace which may prove helpful to the person praying. Only one grace should be proposed for a single prayer time. Some of the graces I propose most frequently are as follows:

'At the beginning of your next time of prayer (and at other times when you think of it), I'd like to suggest that you:

➤ ask Jesus to help you to draw closer to him.
➤ ask God to deal with anything in you which *may* be hindering his approach to you.
➤ ask God to help you to trust him more.
➤ ask God to deal with the fears/anxieties/hurts you've described to me.
➤ ask God to show you *whatever* he wants you to see or understand.
➤ ask God to clarify for you *whatever* it is he may be asking of you.

It is important to propose fairly *general* graces such as the above, rather than specific ones. This is partly because it is not helpful to put into the person's mind the idea that there is just one particular thing God should be showing her or doing within her. And partly it is because *you* cannot know for certain what God wants to do with her. The type of graces suggested above do not tell God exactly what to do or how to do it; rather, they enable the person to hold areas of need up to God, leaving *him* to deal with the individual in the way he knows to be best.

Food for the Journey

Offering a person a scriptural passage with which to pray is a bit like offering her manna from heaven. Just as the Israelites, when they first went out to gather the white stuff, asked 'What is it?', so also the person you are guiding may initially feel uncertain of the value of praying with Scripture. However, if she takes the time and the trouble to pick it up and 'consume' it in reflection and imaginative contemplation, she will find that it is indeed nourishment given by God himself, and that in it she is privileged to encounter him.

9

Dealing with Potentially Difficult Situations

'Lord, save us, we're sinking!'

I sat looking across at Jane, a late middle-aged woman who was as singularly unattractive as one could imagine. She was outwardly dowdy, the expression on her face was ugly, and she was abusing me for having invited her to come on the retreat. Had anyone been listening to her monologue, that person might have been excused for thinking that I was the source of all her problems and totally to blame for her present state of mind. My own state of mind was, I confess, not lily white. As is my wont, I was conscious of the Lord with me in the situation, but the arrow prayer I shot heavenwards at that moment was something like 'HELP! You're going to have to work a miracle here, Lord, because I just want to give her a piece of my mind and send her packing!'

Well, to my astonishment, almost as soon as I had sent up that cry for help, I suddenly found myself looking on Jane with immense tenderness, love and compassion. And not only had my attitude and emotions been transformed, but I also found myself speaking to Jane words of great hope and encouragement – words I would have been incapable of think-ing a few moments before. Then, as she felt and heard this positive response, the harshness and anger gradually left her face, and she began to speak positively about what the Lord might have in store for her. She left that session in a changed frame of mind and went on to make a very fruitful retreat.

At times, new prayer guides can feel uncertain how to deal with poten-tially difficult or awkward situations which may come up in a prayer guidance session. Guides differ one from another with regard to *what* they find particularly awkward or difficult, but by examining in this chapter some of the sticky situations which might arise and proposing possible ways of dealing with them, some sense will hopefully be given of the underlying principles involved.

Basic Guidelines for Dealing With Difficult Situations

When confronted with a difficult situation during a prayer guidance session, it is worth following five basic guidelines:

1 **Send up an arrow prayer** asking the Lord to inspire all your thoughts and reactions and to guide your response to the person and/or situa-tion.
2 **Have Confidence** in the Lord's ability to help you deal with the situation adequately.
3 **Do not show surprise** at anything said, nor uncertainty as to how to respond. A moment of silence while you pray and reflect on an appro-priate response is perfectly acceptable, as long as you have made a *sympathetic* 'hmmm' to indicate that you have indeed heard.
4 **Keep in your mind** the basic question: 'What is the Lord trying to do with this person, and how does her attitude or what she is sharing affect her relationship with him?'
5 **Do not try to 'correct'** anything in the person's attitude or experience yourself. It is fundamental to this method that you enable the person

to receive directly from the Lord whatever healing, insights or experience may be needed.

The following describe some of the situations or awkward moments a prayer guide might occasionally encounter while guiding others in a retreat or Week of Guided Prayer, together with a few suggested strategies which might prove helpful or effective.

Situations Reflecting the Attitude or Mental State of the Person

1 The person shows signs of being deeply disturbed, mentally ill or extremely emotionally unbalanced

In cases of mental illness or considerable emotional imbalance, especially if it seems to you that the person might be prone to hearing 'voices' or hallucinating, you should *not* propose imaginative contemplation. As discussed in Chapter 8, a simple psalm, the rosary or the Jesus Prayer are generally safe to use in such cases.

2 The person clearly does not wish to co-operate with the method; for example the person simply wants you to 'tell him what God wants of him', but is unwilling to spend the allotted time in prayer

This is one instance in which there is very little you can do to help the person. You may want to explain to him that unless he spends time in prayer, he will be unable to hear what God wants of him, and that your task is simply to help him to process what he experiences in his prayer. It may help to send the person out with another passage or two to pray with, but if he still fails to do so, you will need to explain, courteously and gently, that there is nothing further you can do to help him.

3 The person is largely focused on deep-seated resentments or woundedness for which she does not seem to want healing

Occasionally, a person may begin a retreat or Week of Guided Prayer, but spend every prayer time and guidance session reiterating and recounting all the hurts and suffering she has experienced in the past. Sometimes this may amount to an obsession from which *she does not actually want to be set free*. The most effective way to begin to help such people tends to be to ask them directly whether they would like to be free of the resentment or woundedness they are feeling.

If they don't, they will typically avoid answering the question and start telling you yet again all about the source of their hurt. It might help gently to repeat the question, but if they are still unable to give you a clearly genuine 'yes', it is possible that you may not be able to help them very much. The best you can do is to point out that by remaining focused on the hurt, they are *harming themselves* – something God clearly doesn't want for them. You might then suggest that they ask God to free them from the 'after-effects' of what they have suffered, and give them a passage or two in which they may ask for this healing, such as the woman who touched the cloak of Jesus (Mark 5.25–34), blind Bartimaeus (Luke 18.35–43), or the healing of the paralytic (John 5.1–15).

If, however, they say they *do* want to be free, then your task is much easier. You can ask them to pray for the grace to be set free from their resentment or woundedness, and suggest that they use the same sort of passages referred to above.

4 The person expresses resistance to the methods taught as being 'unbiblical'

It might help to remind the person of the clear biblical teaching that God has created us in his image and likeness (Genesis 1.27), which means that every faculty we have is good and can be used by God to speak to us and encounter us. You might also remind the person that God has often spoken to people through dreams, which are the imagination flowing from the unconscious (Matthew 1.20–21 and 2.13), through stirring the emotions (see examples in Chapter 7), and through the imagination we know as 'visual memory', when, for example, Jesus reminded Nathanael of a clearly meaningful incident under a fig tree (John 1.48–49).

5 *The person has not taken his prayer time or has not completed it*

It is a good idea gently to explore with the person *why* he didn't do these things. It might be the result of a genuine crisis or emergency, but more often it is that the person has either not given the prayer time priority over other things he wanted to do, or that he felt bored and quit early. These are very common temptations! It might help to remind the person that 'entertainment' is not the purpose of prayer, and that as he has *promised* that time to God, a failure to give it is rather like snatching back a present one has offered to a friend – a discourtesy few of us would consider doing to another human being. How much less should we do it to God! You might suggest that the person pray very specifically for the grace to make the time for his prayer. (Praying for this grace will be equally helpful if, as is possible, the failure to take his full prayer time is due to an inner resistance of some sort.)

6 *The person shares an excessive amount of visual imagery which occurred during her prayer time*

There are people who are prone to receiving visual images at random, and not all such images are significant. There are also persons who simply 'play' with their imagination during their prayer time, without using the Bible passage to guide it. One might ask a person whether she can see any particular significance in the specific images – that is, whether they are symbolic of something in her life or her relationship with God. If not, it is usually better to leave the images to one side and try to discover what stood out for the person when she read and reflected on the passage itself. The questions listed in Chapter 7, under 'Identifying the Heart of the Experience', could prove helpful in doing so.

7 The person is able to enter into imaginative contemplation, but reports that she was unable to draw near to Jesus, or that Jesus refused to look at her, turned his back on her, or wasn't even aware of her presence

Such an experience does not, of course, accurately represent the attitude of the Lord towards this person, but it does suggest that the person may possibly be harbouring an image of God as a being who is not loving, but, instead, judgmental and punitive. It is also possible that the person may be feeling some sense of guilt (even if she is not guilty of anything), or some resentment because of 'what God has done to me' (using God as a scapegoat for sufferings in life). At the very least, such an experience would suggest that this person is not aware at 'heart level' of God's immense love for her.

It's a good idea to try to help the person identify whatever such feelings may underlie her image of God, and to suggest a passage for her next prayer time in which she may experience God's love for her. If she has found it difficult to approach Jesus, a passage such as Luke 19.1–6, in which Jesus takes the initiative, might help. You should suggest, as a 'grace to pray for', that the person ask the Lord to remove anything which could be hindering her approach to him (or his to her), and you should encourage her to talk with Jesus or God the Father about anything she's aware of which may be holding her back.

One thing you must *not* try to do is to 'correct' the sense of guilt or the resentments yourself. As has been pointed out above, it will be far more effective if the person receives healing and/or a new perspective *directly from the Lord in prayer.*

8 The person reports that she couldn't focus on the prayer, that she had lots of distractions, or that there was some problem or worry occupying her mind

We all have distractions in prayer! The best strategy for coping with them is gently to bring the mind back to the passage or to the Lord himself. The person should not waste time and energy 'fighting' the distractions. If, however, she reports having one particularly persistent distraction, you might well advise her to 'take the distraction to Jesus', and to ask him to show her if there is something to be learnt from it. The distraction may, for example, indicate an underlying 'unfreedom' with which the Lord is wanting to deal. In such a case, or when there is a particularly strong fear, worry or problem involved, it is important that, even while holding it up to the Lord, the person's main focus be primarily on *him* – not on the distraction, problem or fear.

Dealing with distractions is dealt with in Chapter 3, and the diagrams there can be used to illustrate the point. (But make sure that the person is not expecting instant results. God does not work according to human timetables!)

9 The person uses something which came up in his prayer to justify a selfish or vengeful attitude or behaviour

Occasionally a person may misinterpret the insight or experience received during his time of prayer in order to justify his anger, resentment or harsh behaviour towards another person. (See the example at the beginning of Chapter 5.) Such a misinterpretation can typically be recognized by a lack of peace and tranquillity in his choice of words, his facial expression and his tone of voice, and by evidence of a 'hard' and perhaps vehement attitude. It is important to help the person to recognize the difference between the 'satisfaction' he may feel at that point (a false peace deriving from self-justification or self-complacency, which does *not* come from God) and the genuine loving and forgiving peace which is the mark of the Lord's working within him.

10 The person speaks impersonally of what the Lord says to 'us', or of the love of God for 'everyone', or what 'you' experience, etc.

Such language, avoiding any reference to himself, may indicate that the person does not actually feel loved by God, or has not personally experienced God's presence. Alternatively, the person may simply feel that it would be arrogant to think that God would speak to him individually. It may help to say something like 'Let's focus on what the Lord is trying to say to *you* at the moment.' Or, at times, it may be worth asking the person to repeat what he has just said, but in the first person. If he finds it very difficult to do this, it could be helpful to suggest that he pray, at the beginning of his next prayer time (and at other times whenever he thinks of it), for the grace of a deep experience of God's love for him *personally*.

11 *The person is interpreting the passage as a message for someone else (such as her spouse, son, friend, etc.)*

As with the similar situation described in 10, you should guide the person back to the meaning for *her* of what happened in the prayer time, saying something like 'Let's focus on your *own* relationship with God. Can you identify what the Lord was trying to say to *you* through this reading?' It may help to remind the person that she cannot truly help anyone else *unless and until she herself has been helped by God*, and also that it is essential to leave God to deal directly with others. What the person needs to do is to hand those others over to God in simple trust.

Situations to Do With Method

12 *The person reports that* nothing *has happened during her prayer time*

Something will have happened! Frequently the problem is only that the person had some specific expectation which prevented her from recognizing the experience God actually chose to give her. (See the case cited at the beginning of Chapter 6.) Ask the person to describe to you step by step how she passed the half-hour and, as you listen, emphasize the significance and importance of what *did* happen, whatever that was. Even if *you* are unable to perceive much of anything happening, it is important to affirm the fact that the person gave that time to God, and that God will have used it, even if only at the level of her unconscious. You might like to suggest that in her next prayer time she ask for the grace to perceive what the Lord is wanting to do with her or say to her.

13 *The person didn't make any notes on the prayer time*

Ask if the person took time to reflect on the prayer experience after-wards. Remind him of the importance of doing so and of writing down briefly at that point (but not *during* the prayer time) what happened and what seemed significant. (See the 'fourfold dynamic' described in Chapter 2.) Remind him that writing a few notes is an important part of the process, as God will often give him fresh insights as he does so. It's a good idea for the person to bring his notes when he meets with you, in order to help him remember details he might otherwise forget.

14 *The person is simply reading her notes to you*

It is important that the person *tell* you what happened, without simply reading from her notes, as this will give you a far better idea – from her tone of voice, facial expression and body language – what the 'feel' of the prayer time was. As has been discussed in Chapter 5, this is impor-tant information for discerning just what has or has not clearly come from God.

If the person finds this difficult, you might suggest that she read a section of her notes silently, then look up and give the gist of what she has just read. It's also worth checking that she has not been writing notes *during* the prayer time, but only in the time of reflection after-wards. Writing *during* the prayer time negates the purpose of the prayer – which is listening! (See **17**, below.)

15 *The person is describing in excessive detail everything that happened in the prayer time*

Check that the person is not writing notes *during* the prayer time, but only in the time of reflection afterwards, and remind him of the importance of sorting out 'the wheat from the chaff' as he does so, by identifying the most significant, moving or striking moments. Explain that it is more helpful to you if he shares with you relatively briefly, highlighting these points. Some people may need to go through their notes immediately *before* their meeting with you in order to do this.

16 *The person reports not having been able to imagine anything at all*

Some people find it difficult to trust the method of using the imagination in prayer. If the person demonstrates some such block over imaginative contemplation it may prove helpful to remind her that this use of the imagination has nothing to do with fantasy (i.e. make-believe which is *not* grounded in truth), as what we are doing is employing this God-given faculty in the service of our faith – that is, in the service of truth. (See 'Teaching Imaginative Contemplation', Chapter 3.) God is well able to guide our imagination if we allow it. The person might usefully be reminded of the importance of offering her imagination to the Lord at the beginning of each prayer time, and of asking him to protect it from other influences.

If the person claims not to have any imagination, remind her what would go on in her mind if a loved one were to go missing! (*Everyone* has imagination!) You may need to explain how important this type of prayer can be for those who genuinely want to hear God speaking to them. It is the most accessible way of encountering the Lord face-to-face in the twenty-first century. It can sometimes help the person if you lead her in a very brief imaginative prayer exercise then and there – during the guidance session – to show her how simple it is.

17 *The person has evidently spent time during his prayer, rather than afterwards, analysing his experience of the passage, and/or writing notes*

It can be helpful to give the analogy of a meeting with a friend, *during* which one wouldn't waste time going off to analyse the conversation or write notes about it! One would remain with the friend, simply and naturally enjoying his or her company.

It could also be helpful to remind the person to trust in the Holy Spirit to bring to his mind afterwards anything of real importance (cf. John 14.26).

18 The person has evidently spent her prayer time analysing the passage, rather than experiencing it

It's a good idea to ask *how* the person prayed with the passage, and to remind her of the difference between 'Bible study' and 'praying with the Bible'. If she prayed with a *lectio divina* passage (such as a Psalm, a prophecy, words from an epistle or teachings of Jesus), ask what words or ideas stood out for her, and what emotions she felt. It can sometimes help, when a person is overly analytical, to give her an exceptionally short passage (perhaps just one verse) with the suggestion that she spend time just repeating it, savouring every word, and noticing any emotions it stirs up. Remind her of the importance of conversing with the Lord about any thoughts or emotions which may surface.

If it was an 'event' passage with which the person prayed, did she invite the Lord to use her imagination before trying to enter into the event imaginatively? If so, what actually happened during the time of prayer? It may be simply that she is reluctant to share what happened for fear that it will be seen as childish fantasy. Your encouragement could be vital in such a case.

In the case of a person who seems unable to get away from analysis of the passage, it can help to tell her *not to open her Bible at all in the next prayer time*, but rather to enter into a biblically based scene which you describe to her. For example:

'You will find yourself in a wilderness place. Get in touch with your own feelings and needs, and then wander along until you find a bush or tree under which to sit. Then ask/allow God to come to you in some way, and see what he says or does. Remember to share with him your own needs, and to listen to anything he may say to you in reply.' (Based on 1 Kings 19.1–8.)

I have known this approach to yield very moving and remarkable results.

19 The person reports that he was able to live the event
imaginatively up to a certain point, but that he then got stuck and
couldn't imagine anything more

In such a case it may simply be that he had had the experience God wished to give him in that particular prayer time. What he experienced may have been enough. You may like to explain to him that God often gives us only a very brief snippet of an imaginative experience, and then leaves us to remember it and reflect on it for the remainder of the prayer time. The person's dialogue with God can continue even after the imaginative experience seems to have ended.

Occasionally, however, getting stuck partway through a prayer time may indicate the presence of some resistance within the person. It can be worth exploring this by asking how he felt at the point when he got stuck. If he was aware of any fear or resentment towards God, or any unwillingness to continue, it could be helpful for him to pray for healing of that fear, resentment or unwillingness, and the grace of complete openness to God's approach. If not, it might help him to pray for the grace to trust and find meaning in whatever experience God sends. (Recognizing and dealing with possible resistance is dealt with more fully in Chapter 5.)

Other Situations

20 The person has prayed with the wrong passage

On one occasion, I had suggested that someone pray with Psalm 139, omitting the 'cursing verses' 19–22. The person misread her notes and prayed *only* with verses 19–22! I was surprised to hear her sharing how the Lord had managed to convey something positive even through those unlikeliest of verses!

So if you find that the person has prayed with the wrong passage, don't panic, and don't make her feel foolish! You can just say that that wasn't the passage you had intended, but that God will have used it any-way. Have a quick read through the passage she *actually* prayed with (so as to be able to identify what did and did not speak to her), and then listen to her experience as usual. (It will not necessarily be helpful or appropriate to give her again the passage you had actually intended. Be guided by the usual considerations for choosing texts, as explained in Chapter 8.)

21 *The person sheds tears while sharing her prayer experience with you*

It is not at all unusual for people (including men) to shed tears during a retreat or Week of Guided Prayer. This is due to the more intense encounter with the Lord which the Ignatian method facilitates, taking the person deeper into her heart. One sign that this has happened is that the emotions are nearer the surface. So it is very important simply to allow a person to cry, without attempting to 'comfort' her, and without trying to hurry her back to her verbal sharing. Simply *be there* for her, making 'compassionate sounds' if appropriate, and perhaps offering a tissue. *Don't*, however, say anything like 'That's right, let it all come out' – which for some people is a real turn-off. If the person apologizes for weeping, it is best to say something like 'That's OK; it's not at all unusual for people to cry during a retreat or Week of Guided Prayer. This is because we tend to be more in touch with our emotions when we are in closer contact with God, so tears can be a very positive sign.'

22 *The person reports praying in tongues*

A person with 'the gift of tongues' may sometimes find himself praying in tongues while praying with Scripture. Provided this is spontaneous, it can be a useful indicator as to which aspects of his prayer experience were most significant, so it can be helpful to discover at what point the 'tongues' surfaced.

If the person shows any uncertainty concerning praying in tongues, the following is fairly sound advice:

✔ The gift of tongues is well known in the Church and is nothing un-usual.

✔ The person receiving the gift is not therefore a 'better person' or 'superior Christian'. (It's even possible he has been given the gift because he is weak and needs strengthening!)

✔ It is a gift primarily for the benefit of the person who receives it, and only secondarily or indirectly for the benefit of others. It should not normally be used in the presence of those who do not pray in tongues, because of the danger of making those people feel inferior or deficient (even though they are neither).

✔ The person who has received the gift of tongues is normally able to exercise it whenever he wishes, and that it is considered important that he do so frequently. It is often an instrument of healing for the person himself, and may also be an effective form of intercessory prayer for others.

23 The person shares something unusual such as an 'out-of-body' experience

Even if the person shares some experience you've never heard of, you should not show surprise or concern. Provided the experience is not a distressing one, it is important to assure the person that it's all right, and that such things do happen from time to time. The experience might not have any significance – unless God is using it in order to give her a new perspective. It's a good idea to ask the person whether she senses that God may have been speaking to her in some way through the experience she has described. If not, and if there is no evident connection with what is going on in her prayer, it is usually best to leave the experience to one side and return to a consideration of whatever else went on during her prayer time.

24 The person shares with you a dream he has had

Occasionally God may speak to a person through a dream (cf. Matthew 1.20–21 and 2.13, as referred to in 4, above), so you should not be too quick to dismiss the dream as having no bearing on the person's prayer. At the same time, however, you should not attempt to *interpret* the dream. You may ask whether the person feels the dream to be significant and, if so, invite him to explain how. It's important to bear in mind the principle that dreams do not normally represent external, objective truth, but only the truth of what is going on within the dreamer's unconscious. A useful criterion in the context of a guidance session is the question 'Does this dream show me anything about the areas in this person which may be most in need of God's intervention?'

25 *You feel disturbed or uneasy as you listen to the person, you feel a dislike for her and/or you find it difficult to maintain eye-contact with her*

It is always important to be aware of your own inner reactions to the person being guided. If you feel in yourself some negative attitude or reaction, you should send up an arrow prayer asking for the grace to see the individual in front of you *as God does*. (Cf. the episode recounted at the beginning of this chapter.) You might also ask yourself *why* you find it difficult to like the person or look her in the eye. It *may* be that you are picking up some spiritual disorder in her (for example, that what she is sharing is not of God, but rather from some other source – the guidelines for discernment are especially important here). Alternatively, you may be picking up a disorder on some other level (e.g. that what the person is sharing with you is not what she has actually experienced, or that she is forming an unhealthy dependence on you or is trying to impress you). You should not, however, judge the person's experience solely on the basis of your own reactions, as the problem may be in you!

26 *The person shows signs of forming an unhealthy dependence on you*

The signs of such dependence can be subtle, but may manifest themselves in the person trying to prolong his session with you, or to make frequent contact with you outside the sessions. Sometimes, you may have a sense of the person hanging upon your every word in a way that makes you feel almost 'devoured'.

This is a tricky situation to deal with, because people who are most prone to forming an unhealthy dependence on their directors are typically the most vulnerable and easily hurt, so extremely gentle handling is essential. The person will need to be dealt with very lovingly, but with the clear goal of disengagement. It may not be advisable to speak of the dependence you see, but you should avoid contact outside of guidance sessions, and it may help the person to adjust if you give him notice that you will not be able to continue guiding him beyond a certain date. If such dependence arises during a short retreat or Week of Guided Prayer, the solution is a bit simpler, as you can simply make yourself unavailable to the person afterwards. (If the person wants or needs follow-up, it is best to refer him to another prayer guide.)

27 The person confesses sin or manifests a sense of guilt

You should never just ignore or skip over a person's confession of sin or expression of guilt. At the very least, you should express compassionate understanding by saying something like, 'Ah yes, it's so easy to fall into that one, isn't it . . .' While you should not 'belittle' the sin or imply that it doesn't matter, you should nevertheless give the person the sense that you are standing alongside her as a fellow sinner.

If she wishes to talk about her sin, you should allow her to do so (briefly, at least), and it is important to assure her that she has received God's forgiveness. If she seems to be feeling weighed down with guilt, it can be a good idea to ask if she feels it would be helpful to receive sacramental absolution from a priest.[17]

Should the person ask to make a formal confession to you, there is nothing to prevent this, though she should understand that you cannot (unless you are a priest yourself) give sacramental absolution. An appropriate response to use if you are not a priest is to turn the words of the absolution into a prayer:

---

17 Many people are under the illusion that sacramental confession is only for Roman Catholics, or that only Roman Catholic priests are willing and able to hear confessions. In fact, most Anglican clergy are well versed in hearing confessions and are very happy to do so, as are some ministers of other denominations.

'I pray that Almighty God may have mercy upon you, pardon and deliver you from all your sins and bring you to everlasting life.'

Alternatively, you might wish to say something like:

'Be assured that God has heard your confession and joyfully forgives you by the power of the Cross.'

(It may be appropriate that such formal confession take place at a time *outside* the prayer guidance session. Apart from avoiding the time constraints in a guidance session, such a separation can emphasize the greater formality and reverence appropriate to the reception of a sacrament.)

28 The person shares a belief which you regard as heretical, or manifests disbelief in some fundamental doctrine of the Christian faith

It is not your responsibility as a prayer guide to correct such errors, if that is what they are. You should continue to treat the person positively and with respect, and to put the best and most charitable possible construction on what he has said. Only if his misunderstanding is having an adverse effect on his prayer relationship with God – or if he specifically asks you about some aspect of the faith – should you comment, and then only very briefly. (You might say something like 'Christians have always believed . . .') In the context of prayer guidance, which is about allowing the Lord to work in the person *directly*, you should never say to him that his belief is wrong. What matters in prayer guidance is helping the person to open his heart more and more to the Lord. In my experience, any deficiencies in what the person thinks or believes will very likely be sorted out as his relationship with the Lord grows and deepens.

Making the Rough Ways Smooth

While our task as prayer guides is not to gloss over the difficulties a person may encounter, nor to help her evade the challenges with which the Lord may be presenting her, we are nevertheless called to minimize or remove any unnecessary obstacles which may be impeding her focus on and attentiveness to the Lord. At times this task may indeed feel like 'making a way in the wilderness', and it will rightly call forth our own unswerving trust and dependence on the Lord to guide us and give us wisdom. But when our efforts to 'make the rough ways smooth' are successful, the results in the person before us will remind us what a noble and worthwhile task we have undertaken.

Appendix 1

Practical Guidelines for Running a Week of Guided Prayer

Setting the Scene

As with any pastoral undertaking, a Week of Guided Prayer needs careful planning to ensure that the participants are not distracted or upset by administrative glitches or lack of forethought. In particular, it is suggested that the following checklist be used.

1 Preliminary Planning

✔ Which prayer guides are able to take part, and how many retreatants is each one willing and able to guide?

✔ Where is the Week of Guided Prayer to be held? How many rooms are available for individual prayer guidance sessions? Is there a suitable room for participants to make themselves tea and coffee, and to chat together while waiting to see their guides?

✔ What are the times of the Initial meeting and the Closing meeting?

✔ Which guide is going to present which parts of the Initial and Closing meetings?

✔ At what time(s) of day are guidance sessions to be held?

✔ Who is to be responsible for:
   – Publicity?
   – Opening the venue and seeing to lights and heating (if necessary)?
   – Refreshments?
   – Allotting prayer guides to participants?
   – Provision and setting up of equipment for the group sessions? this will include items such as:
      Whiteboard and markers.

Overhead projector or PowerPoint projector.
Overhead transparencies or PowerPoint programme.
Paper and felt-tip pens for use by participants.
CD player and suitable CD(s) of quiet, reflective music.
Visual aids such as a rock and a sponge.
Candle(s) and central table or 'altar' for the periods of worship.
Good modern translations of the Bible for loan to those who do
not possess one.
 – Writing up a prayer list of guides and participants for circulation
 among all involved, to enable prayer for one another?
 – Running off the handouts?

2 Publicity

✔ Is the Week of Guided Prayer to be open only to a specific group of
people or advertised more widely?
✔ What is the total number of participants who may be accepted, given
the number each prayer guide is able to guide?
✔ How and where is the event to be advertised?

3 During the Week

✔ What form of supervision will be offered to the prayer guides, and by
whom?
✔ At what time can the prayer guides meet together each day as a group
for prayer and mutual support?

4 After the Week

✔ What sorts of individual 'aftercare' are the prayer guides able to
offer?
✔ Who would be available to oversee an ongoing prayer group, should
participants desire this?

Appendix 2

Guidelines for Distinguishing the Creative from the Destructive*

by Gerard W. Hughes SJ

A Précis of the 'Rules for Discernment' from the *Spiritual Exercises*

1 If the core of our being is **directed to God,** then the decisions we make in harmony with that fundamental desire will resonate in our moods and feelings, bringing some measure of peace, strength and tranquillity. The destructive forces, outside and within us, will oppose this decision that brought us peace, causing agitation, sadness and inner turmoil.

2 If the core of our being is **turned away from God,** any decisions we make, which are in harmony with that fundamental aversion, will comfort and console us, while the creative forces, outside and within us, will trouble us with stings of conscience.

3 **Creative** moods and feelings are to be distinguished from **destructive,** ones not by their pleasantness or painfulness, but by their effect. If going with the mood or feeling leads to an increase of faith, hope and love, then it is creative; if it leads to a decrease of faith, hope and love, then it is destructive.

4 Moods and inner feelings, whether pleasant or unpleasant, that are drawing us towards God, are called '**consolation**'. Painful moods and inner feelings that are drawing us away from God are called '**desolation**'.

---

* This précis is copyright © Gerard W. Hughes, and reproduced by his kind permission. An expanded version with clear explanations is to be found in *God in All Things*, Hodder & Stoughton, 2003, pp. 103–12, and is well worth reading in full.

5 In desolation, we should **never go back on a decision made in time of consolation,** because the thoughts and judgements springing from desolation are the opposite of those coming from consolation. It is, however, useful to **act against the desolation.** We should also **examine the cause of our desolation.**

6 In desolation, remember two things:

a **Know that the desolation will pass.**

b If we can keep the focus of our attention on God, even if we have no felt experience of God's presence, **God will teach us through the desolation.** It is as though in desolation God gouges out our false securities, revealing God's self to our inner emptiness so that God may fill and possess it.

7 **In consolation, make the most of it!** Acknowledge it as a gift, freely given, to reveal a deeper truth of our existence, namely, that we live always enfolded within the goodness and faithfulness of God. In consolation we have had a felt experience of this truth. Let this truth become the anchor of our hope in a time of desolation.

8 **We must face the fears that haunt us.**

Appendix 3

Some Guidelines for Discerning How Best to Serve God

There are three basic steps in discerning how the Lord would have you serve.

1 You need to know and to value your own gifts and interests, and to identify what are the *genuine* options open to you.
2 You need to spend enough time in prayer to reach a position of 'inner freedom' concerning the options open to you – that is, to be genuinely willing to do whichever may be to the greater glory of God (and therefore the fullest service of others). (A spiritual director can be especially helpful with this step.)
3 You will then be in a position to follow objective guidelines to determine which of the options will indeed be to the greater glory of God (and therefore the fullest service of others).

When you have reached the third of these steps, the following considerations may help you in your discernment.[18] (In each section, the points are listed beginning with the most important.)

Where to Serve: If you have a choice concerning where to serve, you might ask yourself the following questions:

- Where is the greater need?
- Where is your service likely to be most productive?

---

18 These considerations were compiled jointly with Enid Morgan SGS, based on the *Jesuit Constitutions*, paragraphs 622–626, and are reproduced here with her kind permission.

- Where is your service likely to be well supported?
- Are there people in each place who could be trained to continue the work?

The Nature of the Service: If you have two or more types of service you could undertake, the following considerations might help you:

- Work for the spiritual welfare of others would normally take priority over work for their physical welfare, unless the latter need is especially urgent.
- Which type of service is most needed?
- Are you the only person who can do one of the types of service?
- Preference should normally be given to:
  - Work which can be done safely, easily and quickly.
  - Work which will achieve most good.
  - Spiritual work of lasting value.

Suitability for the Task: It will be helpful to consider whether you are equally suited to the work involved in each form of service. Different qualities and skills are needed for different tasks:

- Strength and health for physical work.
- Spiritual maturity and discretion for spiritual guidance.
- Ability to teach and lecture for training others.
- Confidence for speaking to large audiences for evangelism.
- Ability to work harmoniously and well in a team, if working alongside others.
- The support of a colleague if you work better with such support.
- A balance of abilities if working with others.
- Shared vision and aims with the people involved.

Preparation: It is wise to consider whether each of the options will allow for the following:

- Proper instruction and training for the task, if such is needed.
- Adequate help and support from colleagues and superiors as you get started.
- Adequate financial support, if this is a consideration.

Length of Time Given to the Work: Once you have embarked on a form of service, you will need to consider how long to continue it. Factors which may influence this are:

- Is a need being met?
- Is the work successful?
- Are there more important opportunities in other places?

Appendix 4

Some Scripture Passages
Suitable for Prayer

God's Love for Us

Isaiah 43.1–7	Fear not, you are mine.
Isaiah 46.3–4	I am he who will sustain you.
Isaiah 49.13–17	I have engraved you on the palm of my hand.
Hosea 2.16–25	I will speak to your heart.
Matthew 11.28–30	Come to me . . . my yoke is easy.
Luke 18.15–17	Jesus blesses the children.
Ephesians 1.3–14	The Father has chosen us in Christ.

Trust in God / God's Care for Us

1 Kings 19.1–8	Rise and eat, lest the journey be too much for you.
Psalm 23 (22)	The Lord is my shepherd.
Psalm 27 (26)	The Lord is my light and my salvation.
Psalm 139 (138):1–18	You have searched me out and known me.
Isaiah 35	The desert shall blossom.
Isaiah 41.8–13	Do not be afraid, I will help you.
Isaiah 55.1–3 and 6–11	Listen to me and your soul shall live.
Jeremiah 29.10–14	I know the plans I have for you.
Ezekiel 34.23–28	I will shepherd them and make a covenant of peace.
Habakkuk 3.17–19	The Lord is my strength.
Mark 4.35–41	Jesus calms the storm.

Luke 10.38–42	Martha and Mary.
Luke 12.22–32	Behold the lilies of the field.
John 7:37–39	Let anyone who thirsts come to me.
John 14.23–27	The promised Holy Spirit / My peace I leave you.
Romans 8.31–39	Nothing can come between us and God's love.

Repentance/God's Forgiveness

Psalm 51	Have mercy on me O God.
Ezekiel 36.23–28	I will give you a new heart.
Hosea 14.2–9	Return to the Lord your God.
Matthew 9.10–13	I came to call not the righteous, but sinners.
Luke 7:36–50	Woman who was a sinner anointing Jesus' feet.
Luke 15.11–24 (or 11–32)	The prodigal son.
John 8.1–11	Woman caught in adultery.
Hebrews 12.1–13	Let us lay aside every weight and sin.

Forgiving Others

Matthew 5.20–26	First go and be reconciled with your enemy.
Matthew 5.43–48	Love your enemies.
Matthew 7:1–5	Judge not, lest you be judged.
Luke 23.33–34	Forgive them, for they know not what they do.
1 Corinthians 13.4–13	Love forgives all things.

Healing

Ezekiel 47:1–12	The river flowing from the temple.
Luke 5.17–26	The paralytic let down through the roof.
Luke 8.43–48	The woman who touched the robes of Jesus.
Luke 18.35–43	The blind man of Jericho.

The Lord's Call to Follow Him

Exodus 3.1–6	The burning bush.
Isaiah 6.1–8	The call of Isaiah.
Isaiah 49.1–7	The Lord called me before I was born.
Matthew 14.22–33	Jesus calls Peter to walk to him on the waters.
Mark 10.17–22	The rich young man.
Luke 4.16–21	The Spirit of the Lord is upon me.
Luke 5.1–11	Call of the first four disciples.
Luke 9.23–26	Take up your cross and follow me.
Luke 10.1–9	Jesus sends out the seventy-two disciples.
Luke 19.1–10	Jesus calls Zacchaeus down from the tree.
John 1.45–51	When you were under the fig tree, I saw you.
John 13.1–15	Foot washing – as I have done to you . . .
John 15.1–17	I am the vine, you are the branches.
2 Corinthians 6.1–10	As having nothing, yet possessing all things.

Our Love for God

Psalm 63 (62).1–8	My soul thirsts for you.
Psalm 84 (83)	How lovely is your dwelling place, Lord of hosts.
Song of Songs 2.8–14	The voice of my beloved.
Matthew 13.44–46	Treasure hidden in a field / pearl of great price.
Mark 12.28–34	The greatest commandment.

Praise and Thanksgiving

Psalm 100 (99)	Sing to the Lord, all the earth!
Isaiah 61.10 to 62.5	He has clothed me in the garments of salvation.
Luke 1.46–55	Magnificat – the Song of Mary.
Luke 1.68–79	Benedictus – the Song of Zachariah.

Miscellaneous

1 Kings 19.9–13	The still small voice.
Matthew 5.1–12	The beatitudes.
Matthew 17:1–8	The transfiguration.
Luke 24.13–35	The road to Emmaus.
John 1.1–18	In the beginning was the Word.
John 20.1–10 (or 1–18)	The empty tomb/encounter with Mary Magdalene.
John 21.1–14	Breakfast with the risen Lord.
Philippians 3.7–16	All this I count as loss / I press on to the goal.
Philippians 4.8–13	I can do all things in him who strengthens me.

Appendix 5

Reported Prayer Experiences on Which to Practise

The following are hypothetical 'prayer accounts' by participants in a short retreat or Week of Guided Prayer. All of them are loosely and anonymously based on accounts I have actually heard over the years. Although just reading them obviously doesn't give you the information you would gather from the tone of voice and body language, you should nevertheless, be able to identify points of probable significance and aspects which call for affirmation, exploration and/or further teaching. Where there are three dots (. . .), this indicates a brief pause. Where there is a series of dots, this indicates a longer pause, implying strong emotion.

As you read the 'prayer accounts', it might help to ask yourself the following questions:

❖ What is the 'core experience' or 'heart of the encounter' described? In other words, where did the person seem to be closest to or most touched by God? (You might need to ask questions before you can identify this.)
❖ What things might you say and/or ask to affirm or explore the meaning of the prayer time, and at what point would you do so?
❖ What teaching would you give the person about this way of praying?

EXAMPLE:

Hannah: (Mark 3.31–35) 'Well, I read the passage about the blind man who calls out to Jesus. I thought how much courage that must have taken, when he called out in spite of the crowds around him – people telling him to shut up . . . When Jesus came along, he called out and Jesus called him to him. He must have felt pretty good about that. Then Jesus asked him what he wanted. And he said he wanted his sight back. So Jesus gave it to him. That's all that happened, really.'

It appears that Hannah has observed the event, rather than taking part in it, so I would ask 'where she was and whether she was able to be involved in any way'. I would make sure that she didn't feel she'd 'done it wrong', saying just that there's a further step she can now take which will greatly deepen her experience. I would then explain again about 'editing out' the main character, etc.

The one comment which suggests that Hannah felt moved or touched was her sense that it 'must have felt pretty good' to be summoned by Jesus. To help her explore this, I might ask her to close her eyes and spend a minute allowing Jesus to summon her through her imagination. I would then debrief this.

I would suggest that she pray for the grace of a personal encounter with Jesus, and would give her a similar passage for her next prayer time – e.g. Luke 19.1–10 (Zacchaeus) in which Jesus 'summons' her to himself.

1 **Edward:** (Luke 8.43–48) 'This was the passage about the woman who touches the cloak of Jesus. I did what you said and read the passage through slowly. What stood out was that the woman was afraid . . . Then I closed the Bible and tried to imagine myself there. At first it was hard, but then I saw a crowd surrounding Jesus. I didn't really want to go to him . . . but then I suddenly realized he was looking at me over the heads of the people in the crowd . . . . And I couldn't look at him.

I didn't know what to do ... I just wanted to hide. And I couldn't do any more. I'm sorry. I'm no good at praying this way ...'

2 **Barbara: (Psalm 27)** 'I prayed as you told me to with Psalm 27, and it was wonderful! I felt as if the Lord were bathing me with light, light of all different colours, and then I was floating on a sea of warm water which just relaxed me and made me feel good. And as I watched, flowers started bobbing up in the sea all around me, and each one was glowing with a silvery light. And as I lay there, floating on the water, a boat came drifting towards me and I got into it. And I drifted in the boat, looking at the sky and a glorious sunset. And I felt really good ... And presently the boat began to drift up into the sky and came to rest on a cloud. And I looked down at the earth which was all green and blue, and there were lots of birds soaring around me, and one bird in particular stood out, being brightly coloured, like a parrot ... And then I saw a whole lot of colours drifting around between me and the earth. And I got out of the boat and lay back on the cloud and watched other clouds drift past. And then my timer went off so I stopped.'

3 **Charles: (Luke 19.1–10)** 'I prayed with the story of Zacchaeus. And as I'm short myself, I didn't have too much trouble imagining myself in the scene. I saw the crowds coming down the road, and I ran on ahead because I really wanted to see Jesus. And I found a smallish tree – about the size of a large apple tree, easy to climb – and hoisted myself up until I was about 8 feet above the ground. I just wanted to see Jesus as he passed by, but when he turned and looked at me I felt really foolish. Then he passed through the crowd and came over to my tree and looked up at me! I didn't know what to say. He just stood there kind of waiting ... And when I didn't say anything, suddenly he came up into the tree and sat on a branch facing me. I know it didn't happen like that in the passage, but that's how it happened when I imagined it. Was that wrong? ... Anyway, we just sat like that up in the tree, but nothing really happened. And then the half-hour was up.'

4 **Jenny: (Exodus 3.1–6)** 'This was the burning bush passage. I read the passage through, but nothing seemed to stand out. It's too familiar, I suppose. Then, I tried to imagine myself there, but it was hard being

Moses. I've never much liked him, and I don't feel I have much in common with him. But I tried to see the sheep around him, and a mountainous desert region . . . I watched him go up a hill and look at the bush. And I thought about how God shows himself to people in the Bible, and wondered why he used a bush in this story. And then I thought that maybe he chose the bush because it's something ordinary. And I thought about possible explanations for a burning bush and remembered reading somewhere that there are bushes in the desert which will self-ignite, so maybe Moses saw something like that. Anyway, it seemed to me that Moses represented people in exile, and I started thinking about the problem of refugees and asylum seekers in this country. I really don't think the government is doing enough about that, do you? . . . And I went on thinking about this until the half-hour was up.'

5 Harold: (Psalm 139.1–18, 23–24) 'I was praying with Psalm 139, and I had some strange experiences. I read it slowly, trying to understand each verse, and several of the verses really stood out for me. I didn't much like the idea of God spying on people all the time. But there was one verse that felt different; that was 'for you created my inmost being'. And I had an image of myself being formed with a sort of glowing innermost core. I'm not sure what that meant. Then, as I was re-reading it I was struck by the phrase 'all the days ordained for me were written in your book', which seemed to refer to my death. And another verse which struck me was 'darkness is as light with you'. And also 'your works are wonderful'. Oh yes, and another thing which seemed important was 'such knowledge is too wonderful for me'. And also, 'Search me, O God, and try my heart', though I didn't like this too much. I suppose everyone feels scared at being seen by God. I remember my grandfather talking about the big EYE that used to be posted in pubs and other public places to remind people that God was watching them all the time. I think that really must have given people the creeps . . .'

6 Tracey: (Exodus 3.1–6) 'When I prayed with this passage . . . about the burning bush . . . I had a rather amazing experience . . . I found myself in a desert location just about sunset, and the whole surrounding area, which was hilly, was bathed in golden light, with dark shadows in the ravines and valleys . . . And there was a sheep standing near me who

kept looking at me . . . and it seemed to know me. Well, I was just standing there, gazing at the sheep, when I noticed a pinprick of light on the
hillside opposite me. And at first I thought it was just something shiny
on the ground reflecting the last rays of the sun. But then I realized that
it was getting larger. And I started climbing down to cross over to it. It
was rough going, on account of all the rocks strewn around, and at one
point there were three rocks nestled together as one, fitting one another
perfectly . . . in a way that's hard to describe. They were sort of flecked
with gold. As I got nearer and started climbing the hillside where I'd
seen the light, the brilliance of it increased, until I could barely look at
it. Finally, as I got really close I had to shield my eyes as I walked.
Suddenly, I stopped, because I had heard a kind of spine-tingling noise
– a bit like a high note played on a violin. I started moving forward again
towards the bush, and suddenly felt awe-struck, as if I'd strayed into
someplace very posh where I didn't really belong. And I felt the ground
tremble beneath me, . . . and I sank down on to my knees and hid my
face . . . . And I was in tears . . . I don't know why . . . .
I'm sorry . . . . It was so beautiful, I couldn't look at it . . .
And that was all I could do. There wasn't any more.'

7 James: (Isaiah 49.14–16) 'When I read this passage, I felt really angry.
Those words 'The Lord has forsaken me' felt so true, and I thought of
all the horrible things that he's allowed me to suffer. And I spent quite a
while just going over all the hurt and bewilderment I'm feeling . . . It
wasn't until I read on to the next verse, that I realized what the passage
was saying. I still couldn't altogether believe it, that the Lord never for-
gets me. It doesn't feel like that. But I was trying to believe it. My mind
was wandering quite a lot. And I don't think I really got much out of the
prayer time. I wish God *did* care for me the way this says he does. Why
do you think he makes me suffer so much? Where is he when I need
him?'

8 Helen: (Luke 19.1–10) 'This was about Zacchaeus climbing a tree. I
read the passage through, and what struck me was that Jesus paid any
attention to such a despicable piece of humanity as Zacchaeus. I was
thinking that I wouldn't have looked at him twice, and I certainly
wouldn't have risked ruining my reputation by going to his house and

eating with him . . . When I started to pray with the passage imaginatively, I found myself walking alongside Jesus in the midst of the crowd.
And I saw him look over to a tree beside the road and to the little man
in it and I hoped he wouldn't stop. But he did, of course, and I felt really
jealous as he went right over to the tree and told Zacchaeus to come
down. There I was in the crowd with him and he didn't invite himself to
my home . . . There was just once that Jesus turned and looked at me.
Anyway, I started thinking about one of my friends who hasn't invited
me to her home for ages. I feel really hurt about that. She never bothers
to ring me up or anything, either. And I decided to ring her up tonight
and tell her just how angry I feel. She should be made to see how horrid
she is . . .'

9 Robert: (Mark 10.17–22) 'I found this a difficult passage . . . It was
the story of the rich man who came to Jesus wanting to know what he
should do with his life. I really identified with him, as I feel so uncertain
of what I should be doing . . . Anyway, I tried to get into the scene, and
set out, in my imagination, to go to Jesus to ask him what he wanted of
me. Only I couldn't find him. I walked all over the place, and he
just wasn't there. So I sat down on a rock and talked to a goat tethered
nearby. (The goat just looked at me as if I were mad.) After a while, it
occurred to me to *ask* Jesus where he was, . . . and suddenly he was there
at my side. I felt a bit frightened and couldn't look at him, but I knew he
was there . . . And I thought about my life and what a mess it seems to
be in at the moment. And I noticed that the valley beneath us was full of
wildflowers, and I could sense their fragrance. That verse 'consider
the lilies of the field' popped into my head. And there was a lovely breeze
. . . And that was all that happened, really.'

Appendix 6

Suggested Responses to the Prayer Experiences in Appendix 5

1 **Edward: (Luke 8.43–48)** I would want to reassure Edward immediately that he seemed to have prayed with this passage very well indeed. It is clear that he has understood how to do imaginative contemplation.

The 'core experience' was clearly the moment at which Jesus looked at Edward over the heads of the people in the crowd, so I would invite him to share a little more about that moment and how it felt. Is he able to say why he couldn't look at Jesus and wanted to hide?

I would want to give Edward a 'grace to pray for' along the lines of '. . . that Jesus may give you the courage to look him in the face', or '. . . that he will deal with anything which may be holding you back from approaching him'. I would not suggest a repetition of the same passage, as Edward sounded a bit fearful about how well he had prayed, and might see that as a request to 'do it better next time', but I would suggest a similar passage, such as Blind Bartimaeus (Luke 18.35–43) or Zacchaeus (Luke 19.1–10), in both of which Jesus actually calls the central character to him.

2 **Barbara: (Psalm 27)** This is an example of someone who is largely 'playing with the imagination', so I would certainly not be tempted to try and interpret the experience symbolically.

Notice that there is only one mention of God. So I would begin by saying, 'I wonder if I might take you back to what you said at the beginning, about the Lord "bathing you with light". Could you please say a bit more about how you envisaged the Lord at that moment?' I might then ask: 'How did you feel about the light with which you were being bathed?' 'Which verse of the Psalm seemed to "trigger" this experience?'

'Were there any other verses which stood out for you?' 'Have you any sense of what the Lord might have been trying to say to you through this part of your experience?'

I might then suggest that Barbara pray with a passage such as Luke 18.15–17 (Jesus blesses the children), asking her to approach Jesus as a little child and ask for his blessing. I would particularly remind her to let her imagination be guided by what happened in the text, though Jesus may have different and very personal things to say to her.

3 Charles: (Luke 19.1–10) The question 'Was that wrong?' would require an immediate brief response, something like 'No, that's fine!' After Charles finished sharing I would say something like, 'Well, it sounds to me as if you have had a very significant experience! We can never predict what Jesus is going to do or say in imaginative prayer, and it's clear that you are able to pray very well in this way.'

I would then focus on the 'core experience' which was the episode from the moment Jesus looked up at Charles until the two of them were sitting up in the tree facing each other. Although no dialogue took place, the very closeness of Jesus to Charles was hugely important. So I would explore this by saying, 'That was pretty amazing that Jesus came up into the tree with you! Could you share with me how you felt at that moment – what emotions were around?' Then, 'What thoughts came to you as you were sitting there with Jesus?' 'Did you have any sense of why Jesus wanted to be with you in the tree?'

I would then say that, as Charles's encounter with Jesus seemed so significant, I wonder whether he would like to return to that tree, to begin to talk with Jesus about whatever is uppermost in his mind and heart. If Charles expressed a preference for a different passage, however, I would suggest another 'encounter' passage, such as 1 Kings 19.1–8, commenting that it might well be Jesus who comes to minister to him under the bush.

4 Jenny: (Exodus 3.1–6) There is some important teaching to be done here, as Jenny tried to 'be Moses', rather than herself, and after a brief imaginative episode she moved into 'Bible study mode'. I would begin, however, by affirming the fact that she was able to imagine the scene, without making any reference to refugees, etc. – unless, in the course

of our discussion, she identified a sense of call to help such people.

As nothing she has said seems to suggest any personal encounter with God, I would then ask 'How did you feel in yourself as you watched Moses approaching the burning bush?' Then, 'Have you any sense of what God might have been wanting to say to *you personally* through this passage?'

I would then remind her of the difference between 'Bible study' and 'praying with the Bible', and explain about 'editing out' the central character and just being there yourself. I would then probably lead Jenny in a short imaginative contemplation using this same passage: 'You are standing all alone on a hillside before a burning bush. Look at it carefully . . . Now you can hear God's voice calling you by your name . . . Listen carefully to hear anything else God may want to say to you . . .' After inviting Jenny to debrief this experience, I would then choose another 'encounter passage' for her next prayer time.

5 Harold: (Psalm 139.1–18, 23–24) Clearly, the 'heart' of Harold's prayer experience was the 'one verse that felt different' and which resulted in a very positive image of himself being formed by God with a sort of glowing innermost core. I would first of all home in on this (leaving aside, to begin with at least, his evident unease about an all-seeing God). I would invite him to share a bit more about how he felt at that moment, hoping to discover whether he had had any sense of being loved by God.

I might then gently explore with Harold his negative feelings about being seen by God at all times, but would not persist if he felt uncomfortable discussing this. I would, however, suggest that he pray for the grace 'to have a felt experience of God's love for him'.

For his next prayer time, I would move Harold into imaginative contemplation, using a passage in which it is the central character who approaches God/Jesus, rather than the reverse (for example, Luke 18.35–43, the blind man of Jericho).

6 Tracey: (Exodus 3.1–6) It is obvious that Tracey has a very fertile imagination, and I would compliment her on the fact, but I would leave aside most of the visual imagery and go on to home in on what was clearly the most significant moment: when she felt the ground tremble

beneath her and was so overcome with emotion. I would ask if she would like to say anything more about that experience. And I would then ask whether she had any sense of why God gave her that glimpse of his beauty. (She probably couldn't say, but I believe it would be worth asking, if only to help her be in touch with the privilege of it.)

Having encouraged her to 'hold on to' such a precious moment, I would probably suggest another passage recounting a divine revelation for her next prayer time; for example, the call of Isaiah (Isaiah 6.1–8, ending it at that verse in order to leave Tracey to have her own, possibly different, dialogue with God). This would potentially deepen the awe-inspiring experience she had just had, while adding other elements which might or might not speak to her and lead her on (a sense of unworthiness, God's cleansing, God's call, and self-offering).

7 James: (Isaiah 49.14–16) This reaction to the passage expressing God's irrevocable love suggests that James is a rather wounded person, and that he hasn't had much, if any, experience of God's love for him. Although I would not comment on this fact, I would gently explore with James the moment at which he 'realized what the passage was saying'. Asking him to articulate the apparent longing he felt, wanting the passage to be true, might help the meaning of it to reach a slightly deeper level within him.

I would ask James to pray for the grace to see the course of his life (including his sufferings) *as God sees it*. And I would give him a passage such as 1 Kings 19.1–8 (Elijah's flight into the desert) or Mark 4.35–41 (Jesus calming the storm) in which God/Jesus ministers to frightened men who felt themselves abandoned by God. I would encourage James to enter into a dialogue with God/the angel/Jesus about his sense of God's having let him down, and to make sure he listens for a reply!

8 Helen: (Luke 19.1–10) Her experience of this passage suggests that Helen is a very insecure person who seems to be concerned about her reputation and popularity and harbours considerable anger. It is telling that she evidently expects her friends to initiate contact, rather than doing so herself.

Without referring to this, I would begin by saying that it sounded to me as if the moment when Jesus turned and looked at her had been the most significant aspect of her experience. I would invite her to share what emotions she had felt at that point, and I might ask whether she was aware of the expression on Jesus' face. If she could have heard him speaking to her at that point, what does she think he would have been saying?

I would gently discourage her from venting her anger on her friend, saying that God is better at dealing with such situations than we are, and I would probably draw the diagram illustrated in Chapter 3, under 'Dealing with Distractions in Prayer'. I would explain that if she focuses on God, rather than her grievances, that will leave God free to deal with them.

I would ask her to pray for the grace of a close and loving encounter with Jesus, and give her a passage which would enable *her* to approach *him* – rather than the reverse. For example, I might suggest Luke 8.43–48 (the account of the woman who sought healing by touching the robe of Jesus from behind).

9 **Robert: (Mark 10.17–22)** I would immediately affirm the importance of Robert's experience with this passage, saying that it seemed to me that quite a lot had happened! I would then comment on the 'core experience' which was the moment Jesus suddenly appeared at his side. And I would invite Robert to share a little more fully about his emotions at that point in the prayer time. I would explore with him whether he had any sense of what Jesus might be wanting for him (hoping that he would recognize the call to *trust* God in the verse which popped into his head). (If Robert failed to make that connection, I would affirm that that verse, and the way it came to him, did indeed appear to be 'of God' and was therefore important to note.)

By way of teaching, I would highlight the fact that Jesus only appeared when Robert thought to ask where he was. This shows the importance of asking God for what we need.

I would ask Robert to pray for the grace to entrust his life – *as it is* – to Jesus. I would probably offer him the option of returning to the same passage, in order to enter into a dialogue with Jesus, but if he expressed a preference for a different passage, I would probably suggest Luke 5.1–11 (the call of Peter), as that contains an element of sorting out one man's life and vocation.

Appendix 7

Some Guidelines for
Ongoing Spiritual Guidance

Although *ongoing* spiritual guidance (or 'direction') is somewhat out-side the scope of this manual, I recognize that those engaged in any form of prayer guidance are frequently asked to serve others in this way. It is not uncommon, for example, for participants in a Week of Guided Prayer to want to continue meeting with their prayer guide afterwards, for regular follow-up support. This may, perforce, involve the prayer guide in regular one-to-one meetings with such persons over a period of some months or even years, to support and encourage their prayer in the context of their ordinary daily lives. For this reason, I offer the follow-ing guidelines.

The Purpose of Ongoing Spiritual Guidance

The purpose of spiritual guidance (or 'direction') on a regular basis over a period of time is to support and encourage the individual in his ongo-ing relationship with the Lord, with particular reference to his prayer and any issues or decisions which may be coming up for him. (The nature of the relationship between director and directee has already been discussed in Chapter 4.)

Beginning With a New Directee

It is a good idea to explain to the intending directee that the first meet-ing will be a 'one-off' so that both you and he can assess whether you are the right person to accompany him in this way. Occasionally you may form the opinion that there is little you can do to help a person, or that you find the person in some way exhausting or off-putting. It is generally unwise to continue meeting with him in either case. You may feel that a person should be seeking psychotherapy or counselling rather than spiritual direction. Alternatively, you may want to suggest that a person establish a more settled way of praying before you begin to meet with him. Or you might want to meet with him once more before deciding.

In any case, you should discuss with the intending directee

- what he hopes for in the relationship and what expectations he may have, and
- your own understanding of what is entailed in spiritual direction.

Some Notes on Method

◆ The frequency of meetings is up to the director and the directee, but my own experience would suggest that, for someone with a fairly active life or ministry, fewer than monthly or six-weekly meetings are not likely to prove adequate. This is because too many 'threads' can get lost or forgotten if the interval is much longer than that. In the case of someone in the process of discerning a call, fortnightly or even weekly sessions could be appropriate, at least for a time.

◆ Given that the director should be helping the directee to discern recurring themes and patterns in what is happening in both his prayer life and his daily life, it is a good idea to ask him to keep a journal. He need not make entries every day, but should write a few notes on any particularly striking or significant experience he may have in prayer, as well as on any important events in his life and/or decisions he is facing. He should then bring this journal to each direction session for reference and to jog his memory.

◆ Most worthwhile direction sessions will include all of the following:
  - A check on how the directee is in general. This may involve physical health, family problems or whatever is uppermost in his mind.
  - A specific look at whatever has been coming up for him in his prayer (which will normally have been affected by whatever is

going on in his life). It is obviously not feasible in this context, however, that he should recount what has happened in *every* prayer time! The 'headlines' are what you need to hear.

– A check on the pattern and discipline of his daily prayer:

  Is he managing an adequate amount of prayer each day?

  How is he spending that time?

  Does he seem to be spending enough time *encountering* God, as distinct from *thinking about* God?

  Is there evidence of an integration between his prayer life and his daily life?

  Is he spending at least some time in Examen each day?

– A gathering together of:

  Some of the things you sense he might do well to pray about (perhaps with an ongoing 'grace to pray for').

  Any suggestions you feel might help concerning his pattern of prayer.

  Any practical steps he might do well to take (e.g. contacting someone who might help in some way, taking his prayer at a different time or place, and so on).

◆ As in the case of prayer guidance in a retreat or Week of Guided Prayer, your aim should be to send the directee away feeling encouraged and positive about his prayer and his relationship with God.

Appendix 8

Materials and Suggestions for Further Reading

Materials

Teaching materials to supplement this book, incorporating much of the artwork in Chapter 3, are available at the following website: www.onholyground.org.uk

Approaching Holy Ground. This CD includes two complete Power-Point presentations (one simpler, and the other more comprehensive) for teaching good prayer method, as well as reproducible handouts for use in Weeks of Guided Prayer, retreats and prayer workshops.

Holy Ground Transparencies. For those who use an overhead projector, a complete set of diagrams and illustrations in the form of overhead transparencies is available. Master copies of reproducible handouts are also included in the pack.

Suggestions for Further Reading

For those who have not made the full *Spiritual Exercises* of St Ignatius, an excellent next step would be to work their way slowly and prayer-fully through the following classic:

The God of Surprises, by Gerard W. Hughes SJ, DLT, 1986

Another excellent classic, if you can get a hold of a copy, is:

Finding God in All Things, by Margaret Hebblethwaite, Fount Paperbacks, 1987

Other books which might prove helpful are:

Soul Friend, by Kenneth Leech, Morehouse Publishing, Revised Edition, 2001
Holy Listening, by Margaret Guenther, DLT, 1993

Index